Editor:
Mary Kaye Taggart

Editorial Project Manager:
Karen J. Goldfluss, M.S. Ed.

Editor-in-Chief:
Sharon Coan, M.S. Ed.

Illustrator:
Kathy Bruce

Cover Artist:
Sue Fullam

Art Director:
Elayne Roberts

Imaging:
David Bennett

Product Manager:
Phil Garcia

Publishers:
Rachelle Cracchiolo, M.S. Ed.
Mary Dupuy Smith, M.S. Ed.

Cooperative Learning Activities for Science

PRIMARY

AF572081

Authors:

Julia Jasmine, M.A.
Grace Jasmine

Teacher Created Materials, Inc.
P.O. Box 1040
Huntington Beach, CA 92647
ISBN-1-55734-659-3

©1995 Teacher Created Materials, Inc. Made in U.S.A.

The classroom teacher may reproduce copies of materials in this book for classroom use only. The reproduction of any part for an entire school or school system is strictly prohibited. No part of this publication may be transmitted, stored, or recorded in any form without written permission from the publisher.

Table of Contents

 ©1995 Teacher Created Materials, Inc.

Introduction

Welcome to the wonderful world of cooperative learning. This book is designed to help primary students learn science skills while being actively engaged in cooperative activities based on the general theme.

A Complete Resource Book

This book provides everything you need to present units using cooperative learning activities. It includes not only innovative classroom techniques but also practical suggestions and blackline masters to help you put the ideas into action in your classroom.

The first sections explain how to make cooperative learning a part of your curriculum. They include an overview, instructions and activities for introducing cooperative learning to your students and parents, guidelines for setting up groups, ideas for a special activity center, and suggestions for assessment and portfolios.

The rest of the book provides a wide range of cooperative activities divided into two parts.

Learning to Be a Scientist develops skills needed in all kinds of science activities: observing, measuring, weighing, reading a thermometer, counting minutes and seconds, guessing and predicting, and making charts and graphs.

Being a Scientist provides opportunities to use the skills learned in the first section in the context of interesting and practical hands-on activities. You may focus on the units that are relevant for your classroom or use them in sequential order.

Easy to Use

This book is designed with the busy teacher in mind. Each activity unit contains a complete lesson plan which explains the **purpose** of the unit, the **skills** to be taught, and the **materials** that are needed, all of which will fit on one cookie sheet for each group. These features will be fully explained in the following pages.

The **procedures** for teaching the unit are described in detail. Ways **to simplify** the unit are provided. These suggestions allow you to adapt the activity to the pre-cooperative learners in a classroom or to shorten the activity to fit into a tight schedule. Ways **to expand** the unit are also provided to challenge advanced students and to continue a lesson that needs further development in the classroom.

A **teacher script** is provided to make framing the activity simple and fun. It is designed to be an aid in addressing the beginning learners. You may choose to use it as is or to modify it to fit your own teaching style.

The lesson plan for each activity concludes with suggestions for **evaluating** and **processing**.

Overview

Cooperative Learning Activities for Science begins the path of science discovery. The book is geared for children who are just beginning to show readiness for cooperative work. The exercises are set in a Science Club context that is fun and easy to understand. Students begin by learning the skills that real scientists use—observing, measuring, weighing, reading thermometers, counting minutes and seconds, guessing and checking, and making charts and graphs. They follow up with interesting, real science activities in which these basic skills are used again and again, while becoming more comfortable with their peers and more knowledgeable about the world around them.

Beginning the Book

To begin cooperative learning on a successful note, focus on the whole-class activities on pages 6–10. In this way, students can begin to interact as a whole class and then in pairs in a non-threatening and positive manner.

These activities will help you build an attitude of friendliness and cooperation in your classroom before attempting to organize student groups. Additionally, whole-class and partner activities will provide you with opportunities for assessing individuals to best determine the members for each group. (See "Selecting Cooperative Groups," pages 11–14.)

Cooperative Learning Groups

This book has been written for a classroom of thirty students, or six groups of five. Simply add or subtract groups, or students in a group, to best serve your class's particular needs. Remember, in cooperative learning, it is best to use an *uneven* number of students in each group whenever possible.

What About Results?

One of the best reasons for introducing cooperative learning activities throughout the curriculum is that children benefit from them in distinctly observable ways. After completing the activities in this book, look for student improvement and mastery in the following areas:

- Oral presentation
- Cognitive and high-order thinking skills
- Communication and conflict-resolution skills
- Self-esteem
- Ability to use science skills
- Understanding of science concepts

How Else Can This Book Be Used?

Besides its usefulness with the beginning learner, this book has many possibilities for use with ESL students. As the concepts are of a beginning nature, children with English as a second language will be helped by the simplified themes of each activity.

 ©1995 Teacher Created Materials, Inc.

Getting Started

How to Start

Cooperative Learning Activities for Science has been designed to help busy teachers combine science concepts and cooperative learning into their regular classroom curriculum with ease. For primary children the mastery of cooperative learning is just beginning, so it is necessary to make any attempt at the cooperative learning process streamlined, and easy to prepare and carry out successfully.

It's Really This Easy!

Each cooperative activity in this book is designed to fit on a cookie sheet. Everything you need can therefore be assembled and placed conveniently in one easily transportable place for each Science Club group. All you have to do is prepare the cookie sheets and, at the beginning of your activity, distribute one cookie sheet with all the materials needed for the experiment to each group. This way you can be free to facilitate the activity, which is such a vital part of the cooperative process.

The Happy Science Club

We have designed this book to revolve around an easy-to-use center. The center for all of these activities is called The Science Club. Your science club center will be a place to store all of your needed materials, to conduct whole-class and large group experiments and activities, a place to meet before and after the activity to discuss what happened, and possibly a place to watch and listen to science-related audio-visual materials. (It is also a great addition to your classroom, fun for children to show off to parents at Open House time, and attractive and colorful for your everyday classroom.)

Getting Organized

Each activity is organized the same way, using the same construct to make your work easier and allow you to get to the most enjoyable part — actually being involved in your students' learning experience! Each activity has the following pages included in this book:

An activity page—This page describes the activity in its entirety.

A cookie sheet layout page—This page gives an actual visual picture of what your cookie sheets will look like for the experiment/investigation.

A group worksheet—This page will be the group worksheet that each cooperative group uses to complete its activity.

A teaching page—This page will give you additional ideas, instructions, or information to facilitate the activity effectively.

An assessment form—Each activity comes with its own individually designed assessment form for you to easily keep track of your students' progress in the activities and enter into their portfolios.

Additionally, some activities will have reproducible blackline masters wherever they are needed to make your job easier!

The Fun in Discovery

We hope that the results of using this book will be to get your students really excited about science from a very early age, as well as to give them some practical logic skills needed for the next phases of their education in science, and the structure for some very important thinking skills. The easy format will give you an opportunity to make your classroom even more exciting and fun.

Whole-Classroom Readiness and Activities

Easing into Cooperative Learning

Prepare your students for cooperative learning by conducting whole-class cooperative activities. Whole-class activities are especially conducive to creating a comfortable, safe environment in which students have some knowledge and understanding of one another. It is helpful to ease into the cooperative experience since many beginning students have never had the experience of cooperative interaction.

Parallel Players and Pre-Cooperative Learners

The younger the children are, the less comfortable they will feel in group situations. Most toddlers and preschoolers parallel play. This means that they play near each other at separate tasks. To begin the transition from parallel play to pre-cooperative learning, teachers can focus on teaching children how to get along. Page 7 offers many activities to facilitate this transition.

Alphabetical Name Game

Secret Secret

Shoe Hunt / Partner Hunt

Concepts such as sharing and taking turns are understood by the pre-cooperative learner, and while a pre-cooperative learner may not always feel comfortable trying to share or take turns, these ideas are ones he or she will recognize. Remember, becoming a cooperative learner is a process. Many adults have yet to master the idea in their work situations. Be aware of your students. When they have had enough of a cooperative activity, turn to a less stressful and more autonomous one.

Partner Play

Cooperation is an important component in any classroom. When children cooperate, they have the opportunity to think about and assimilate new ideas.

Use the whole-class activities on page 9 to nurture the cooperative atmosphere within your classroom. Each activity is followed by a suggested partner play. To help ease your children into the concept of cooperative learning, allow them this time to work with one partner only.

Picture Journal

Rest and Remember

You may wish to have your students become very comfortable with partner play before beginning the cooperative activities in the rest of the book, or you may find it beneficial to use both group and partner activities, depending on your students' learning needs.

 ©1995 Teacher Created Materials, Inc.

Whole-Classroom Readiness and Activities *(cont.)*

1. **Shoe Hunt/Partner Hunt:** Students can use the pattern on page 8 to color two matching shoes. They will write their names on the provided lines. Half the students can then put one "shoe" into a box, bowl, or other container, and leave the second shoe on their desks. The other half will take turns picking a shoe and matching it to the one on the owner's desk. The student whose shoe was picked will then become that student's partner. Each set of partners will talk together to find out three things about one another. They can write the things on the shoes. Use the completed shoes for a bulletin board display.

   This activity is a good icebreaker for shy children or those who do not know each other. Used at the beginning of the school year, it will set the stage for building cooperative teams based on friendly interaction.

2. **Secret Secret:** Choose a leader to begin. Have students stand in a circle. The first person tells the second person a secret. It is then repeated until it reaches the end of the circle and is said aloud. Have the person who began the secret and the person who heard it last compare the differences in the secret. This activity will help students to understand the importance of listening carefully in their cooperative groups.

3. **Walking Through the Neighborhood, I Saw a ...:** This is a whole-class participation alphabet game. Students stand or sit in a circle. Choose someone to lead with the sentence starter, "I was walking through the neighborhood, and I saw a ...." He or she fills in the blank with something that starts with an "A." The next person in the group must think of something that begins with the letter "B," and so on with the rest of the alphabet. (If there are more students after "Z," return to the beginning of the alphabet.)

   You may wish to begin the activity by holding a whole-class discussion about the possible things that a child might see during a walk through the neighborhood. You may also alter the first sentence as desired. For example, you may begin, "In my house I saw a ...," or "I went to the city and saw a ...."

4. **Alphabet Name Game:** Give each student a soup bowl with alphabet macaroni or paper letters. Write a word on the board. The first student to spell the word with his/her alphabet letters is the winner of the round. Next, have students work in pairs to spell as many words as they can with their letters, making a written list of the words they spell. Beginning readers can spell their names by locating the appropriate alphabet letters. This activity increases letter recognition and spelling skills while at the same time introducing friendly competition. (You can also play non-competitively.)

5. **Learn to Take Turns:** Explore the many ways of taking turns. For example, vote, flip coins, let a neutral party decide, draw straws, draw names, guess the number or a letter, or simply take turns being leader.

Whole Classroom Readiness and Activities *(cont.)*

See page 7, "Shoe Hunt/Partner Hunt," for directions.

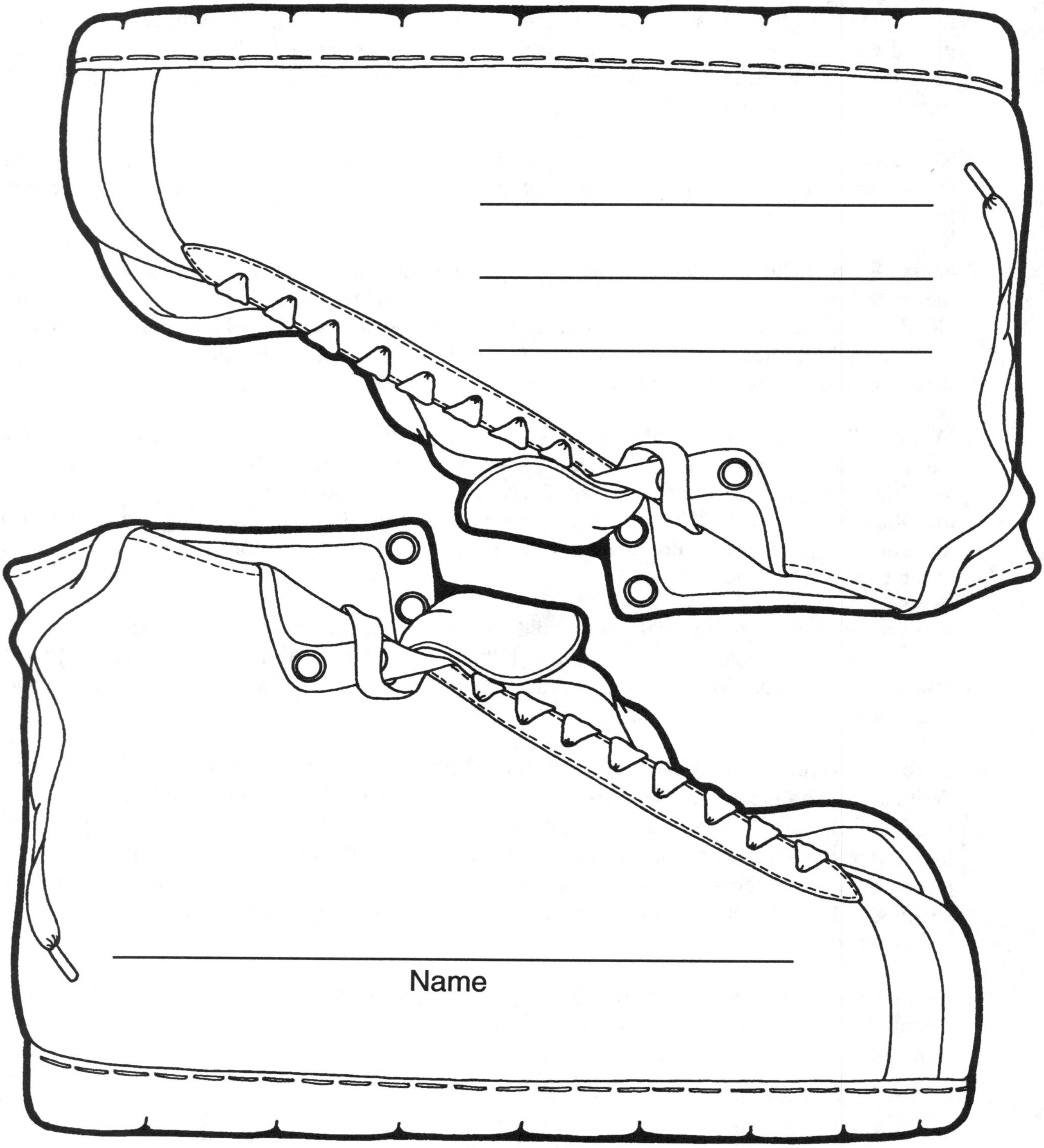

 ©1995 Teacher Created Materials, Inc.

Whole-Classroom Readiness and Activities *(cont.)*

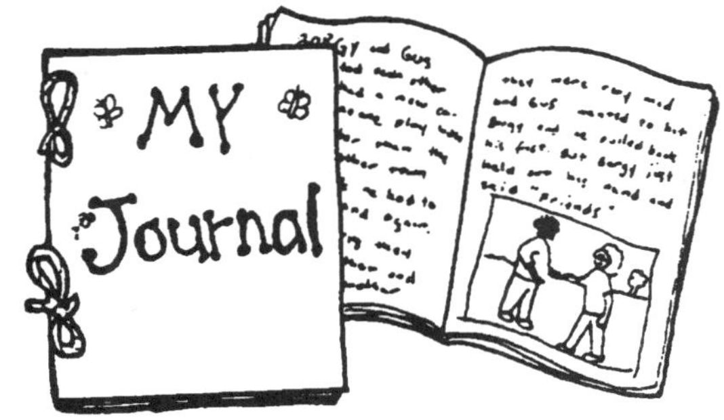

6. **Picture Journal:** This activity can be used for individual and partner interaction. Have each child start a picture journal. When any classroom activity ends, have the children draw and write about the activity. Each journal entry can be dated with a notation about the activity to which it is referring.

   Let the students know that this journal is for them. There is no one right way to do it. It is just for fun. They can look back on it and remember what they did in class and how they felt about it.

   Partners: Assign a partner to each child. Partners will discuss their journal entries. This activity will not only help children relax in a cooperative learning environment, but it will also build cooperative and communicative skills in a nonthreatening way.

7. **Rest and Remember:** This activity will help children prepare for, or unwind after, a classroom activity or special event. Have the children go to their seats and rest their heads on their desks. You may wish to dim the classroom lights or play soft music. While the students are resting, ask them to think about the activity that they just completed. Ask them to picture the activity, see it as a mental movie, and decide what they liked and did not like about it. Ask them how they felt: happy, sad, angry, excited, etc. Ask them what they would like to do differently the next time they work in their groups. You may then wish to follow up by reading the students a short, happy poem or story.

   Partners: Have students talk with a partner immediately following the "Rest and Remember" exercise, discussing what they liked about the activity they have just completed. This can also be another opportunity to use their picture journals.

8. **Letter Home:** This activity is helpful in encouraging language and memory skills. It also engenders parental and parent/child participation in your program.

   Have students write and illustrate, or simply illustrate, what they did in a cooperative learning activity. Use the form on page 10 or have students create their own. Students can then take their letters home.

   Have students return the letters to school and share what their parents thought about the activity and their participation. These letters will also help you to stay in contact with parents consistently, rather than just when there is a problem.

   Partners: Have partners view each other's letters home and make one positive comment or compliment. This activity encourages students to support each other, and it promotes self-esteem.

Whole-Classroom Readiness and Activities *(cont.)*

For directions, see "Letter Home" activity on page 9.

Dear ____

Here is a picture of what my cooperative learning group did today.

I helped my group by:

____

____

____

My favorite part was:

____

____

____

Love,

____

- -

Parent Comments:

____

____

____

Note from the Teacher: Thank you for supporting your child in his/her cooperative learning experience. I welcome all parent volunteers. Please write your number below if you would like a phone call.

Thank you,

____

Name: ____

Name of Child: ______________________________________

Phone: ____

 ©1995 Teacher Created Materials, Inc.

Selecting Cooperative Groups

Kinds of Learners

While all children are different, and certainly children's abilities and skill levels can change, most students fit into one of these four categories of learners:

- High Achievers
- Competent Achievers
- Special Needs Students
- English as a Second Language (ESL) Students

When selecting the members of cooperative groups, be sure to create a mix of all four areas. To help determine the members of each of your cooperative groups, the following descriptions offer some easily recognizable qualities that learners of the same "type" share.

High Achievers

High achievers can fall into two categories. Current educational thought holds that while some students are considered high achievers based on their I.Q., others are labeled this way not so much because of exceptional intelligence but because of exceptional motivation. When looking for the high achievers, consider these qualities:

- High I.Q.
- Problem-solving ability
- Interest in learning
- Multifaceted interests and abilities
- Good verbal skills
- Academic excellence
- Leadership skills
- Good oral communication skills
- Good study and concentration skills
- Exceptional talent

While there are certainly other ways to determine high achievers, and not all high achievers share the same qualities, this partial list will help you know what qualities to consider. High achievers can bring ideas, leadership, and assistance into a cooperative group.

Special Needs Students

While special needs students can be high achievers, low achievers, ESL, or English speaking, the commonality is that they all need special assistance. Some may have difficult family situations, like a divorce or separation, while others may be diagnosed with severe emotional or behavioral problems. While the special needs student requires extra care, placing him/her in the right situation might diminish or solve his/her problem. A sad, distracted child might be placed in a group with a pleasant, happy child, thus giving that child a model for growth. Children, like adults, benefit by the pleasant attitudes of those around them.

Look for these characteristics when determining your special needs students:

- Anger
- A.D.D. student
- Quick frustration
- Low motivation
- Recent family upset
- New to the area
- Recovery from a recent illness
- Low level of socialization skills
- History of emotional or behavioral problems

Selecting Cooperative Groups (cont.)

Special Needs Students (cont.)

While there are other things that may contribute to a child's place in the special needs category, these qualities will give you a guiding framework. Remember that this group, more than any of the others, is transitory. It is very possible during the length of a school year for a child's situation to change enough to either remove him/her from, or add him/her to this category.

English as a Second Language (ESL) Students

ESL students are usually challenged by the circumstances of their learning. Most of us have no idea how traumatic it is to be relocated to a new country with little or no knowledge of the language, the customs, the culture, or the people. Moreover, these students are often without friends, having left their companions behind.

ESL students come in every variety under the sun. Some are extremely well-educated in their own languages, learn English quickly, and assimilate with relative ease. Others have frightening, painful experiences when it comes to success in their new schools.

ESL students have a special place in this book—one that will help you to help them to bring their own cultures into the learning experience. Instead of being ostracized for their differences by other students, they will be able to assume the role of "cultural diplomat." It is the intention of this book to support multicultural awareness and education wherever possible. The emphasis on cooperative learning in each unit makes the challenge of guiding ESL students toward success a little easier. When looking for students to classify as ESL, focus on the following characteristics:

- Recently arrived from another country
- American-born, but in a home where a language other than English is predominant
- Speaks English well, but has not mastered reading or writing in English
- English-speaking, but under the care of one for whom English is a second language
- Remains in the "silent interval" of language acquisition

Once provided with the special attention they need, ESL students often turn out to be competent or high achievers. The cooperative learning activities in this book will help you to access the strengths of these students and to provide them with many self-esteem building opportunities.

Competent Achievers

Unfortunately, competent achievers, often those who "do not give any trouble," just as often get very little teacher attention. In a classroom with 30 or more children, it is the competent child who is "all right" and gets left to fend for him/herself. When identifying competent achievers in your classroom, remember that these children should be rewarded and not penalized for being less demanding. Furthermore, in every group of competent achievers, there are a number of hidden high achievers who will blossom with the proper self-esteem-building attention and experiences.

 ©1995 Teacher Created Materials, Inc.

Selecting Cooperative Groups *(cont.)*

Competent Achievers (cont.)

When looking for competent achievers, watch for the following signs:

- Students you do not often think about
- Oral and written language skills around grade level
- Pleasant low-key personalities
- Low resistance to the learning experience
- Average grades
- Shyness or quietness
- A marked willingness to follow

While not all competent achievers fit this mold, it is at least safe to say that these are the children you are likely to think less about than any of the others. They are the children who stand in line, raise their hands, and rarely cause any disturbances. Competent achievers are the people who keep the world running smoothly, in and out of the classroom, and for this they deserve much praise.

Now What?

Now that you know what to look for in determining the different "learning types" in your classroom, use page 14 to simplify the process.

It may be fun to give each cooperative group a science-related name. For example, the groups might be named after scientists, animals, plants, or elements.

As far as group size is concerned, five is a good number. Therefore, if you have thirty students, you will create six groups, each consisting of five individuals. In cooperative learning situations, an uneven number is an asset during the decision process. (No "hung jury," so to speak!)

Remember The "Salad Bowl"

Rather than as a melting pot, a situation in which everyone's individual traits melt together, the ideal cooperative learning situation should be thought of as a salad bowl. In a salad bowl, all ingredients (individual learning types) mix together. They create synergy while participants remain individuals. Make a cooperative learning salad bowl in your classroom with this simple recipe:

1. Combine the following ingredients: high achievers, special needs students, ESL students, and competent achievers.

2. Select five according to taste. Flavor with the following random differences: genders, personality types, ethnicities, learning styles.

Introduce each ingredient into the mix slowly, stirring in large pieces of humor, understanding, cooperation, and support. Let the mix remain together qualities, strengths, and weaknesses intermingling. Facilitate ingredients rising to the occasion ...and enjoy the results!

Selecting Cooperative Groups *(cont.)*

Legend

HA: High Achievers

SN: Special Needs Students

ESL: English as a Second Language Students

CA: Competent Achievers

Group One *(example)*

(HA)

(CA)

(CA)

(SN)

(ESL)

Notes: ____________

____

____

Group Two

( )

( )

( )

( )

( )

Notes: ____________

____

____

Group Three

( )

( )

( )

( )

( )

Notes: ____________

____

____

Group Four

( )

( )

( )

( )

( )

Notes: ____________

____

____

Group Five

( )

( )

( )

( )

( )

Notes: ____________

____

____

Group Six

( )

( )

( )

( )

( )

Notes: ____________

____

____

 ©1995 Teacher Created Materials, Inc.

Parent Introduction Letter

Dear Parents,

In our classroom this year, we will be approaching the study of science in a very interesting way. We will be learning the skills that scientists use and then applying those skills to interesting scientific investigations. While doing so, each student will have the chance to work cooperatively in pairs or in groups. This will give everyone a chance to take part in many enriching learning experiences.

Here is where you come in. Cooperative learning is a very special kind of learning. Rather than sitting in a chair all day and learning solely by rote, your child will be working in small groups. He/she will have a chance to receive more personalized attention while learning how to interact effectively with peers. Also, as our subject for these units is science, the material studied will be of great interest to the students.

Because of this different way of learning, parent volunteers are very important. If you have several hours a week that you would like to spend in your child's classroom, it would be a wonderful help to the class and it would prove to be a very fond memory for your child.

I realize, of course, that most of you have extremely busy schedules and that some of you will not be able to take part in our classroom activities. However, there are many ways to take part in your child's learning experience, and I would be happy to speak with you about how you can become involved. Thank you for your support!

Sincerely,

____

- -

If you would like me to call you, please fill in the information below and return this bottom portion to me.

Name: ____

Child's Name: ____________________________________

Phone: ____

Assessment and Portfolios

Make It Manageable

Assessing your students' progress does not have to be a formidable task. Included for you here are two handy forms to lighten the load and consolidate your efforts. First, there is the "Individual Anecdotal Record" on page 17. Use this to keep a daily record of individual student progress in each activity or area. Make sure to date these records and to include them in a student portfolio. For more information and other forms, refer to Teacher Created Materials' *Portfolios and Other Assessments.*

Next, you will find "Reflections on the Activity" on page 18. This form is for students to fill out after each activity. Again, store these forms in their portfolios. This form will help you gauge how the students are doing and how they are feeling about the activities.

A Word About Portfolios

Create portfolios out of small boxes or shirt gift boxes, something that can stack but at the same time is big enough for bulky projects. Write the students' names on the sides of the boxes. Students can personalize their portfolio boxes by coloring, cutting out, and gluing the portfolio picture on page 19 to the top of the portfolio box. It is important when assessing your students by the portfolio method to make parents aware that they will not receive as much take-home work. It is always a good idea to make parents aware of your assessment process and make them part of it at the very beginning of the year. Inform them every step of the way and you will save yourself some big headaches. You may even get some interested and wonderful parent helpers!

Assessment and the Pre-Cooperative Learner

Finally, remember that cooperative learning is a difficult concept. Preschoolers and some primary children prefer, and are far better at, parallel play. The transition is usually a slow one. Keep in mind that it is a process and adjust your expectations accordingly.

Have Fun!

This book has been designed with the idea that both you and your students will like the activities and have a good time. Choose activities that you really love. Do not feel you have to do them all or that you must do them word for word. Together with your own creativity, the activities in this book will equal a fabulous year. Good luck!

 ©1995 Teacher Created Materials, Inc.

Assessment and Portfolios (cont.)

Reproduce a stack of these forms and keep them, one for each student in your class, in a three-ring binder. Make your notes right on the appropriate form. When a page is filled up, it can be replaced with a new page and the filled page placed in the student's portfolio. No time is lost transcribing information!

Individual Anecdotal Record

Name ______________________________

Date	Comment

Assessment and Portfolios *(cont.)*

Reproduce this form for your students to use as they start the process of reflecting on their own achievements. This particular form was designed for primary children and requires little writing. Allow plenty of time for the children to look over and think about their work. When the form has been completed, attach it to the work (if possible) and include it in each student's portfolio.

Reflections on the Activity

Name ______________________________ Date ______________

When I look back on the work I have done, I feel...

I have gotten better in...

____

____

____

____

____

I am really proud of...

____

____

Next time I do an activity like this, I will...

____

____

 ©1995 Teacher Created Materials, Inc.

Portfolio Picture

Name____

Happy Science Club—Science Center

Centers Make Sense

In order to keep your cooperative science units running smoothly and to excite your students, we have designed a motivating Science Club Center for you to set up in your classroom. It will help to pull together your science units and provide a storage place for all of your supplies.

Before beginning, look at the list on the next page and see what materials you will need to buy or perhaps have donated from parents or organizations. (See page 23 for a general Parent Supply Letter. We have written this letter so that you can conveniently request whatever it is you feel you need.)

Everything Easy and Organized

This center works in two ways. Its first function is to keep everything you use organized and in place. There is nothing more frustrating than beginning a cooperative activity and finding a crucial part of an investigation is missing. Besides being very frustrating for you, it makes the students unhappy and frustrated, and it ruins the flow of an otherwise enjoyable and successful cooperative activity.

We have written each and every activity in this book to fit on a cookie sheet. Each cookie sheet can be prepared and stored in the Science Club Center. You will want to make children accountable for keeping their Science Club Center neat and usable, and you will find that students become excited about the club theme.

Science Club Fun

The second function of this center is to make the Science Club theme accessible and exciting to your students. Having a place where it all happens is fun for children and certainly showy for your room. In this center, there is a place to conduct experiments, a place to watch science videos and listen to audio tapes, a place to get science books and to read them. All of these things add continuity to the units and importance to the ideas that the students are learning.

What You Need

The following is a list of things that you will need to put this center together. Whenever possible, borrow or ask for donations. There are many things that can be requested from parents. Take advantage of the resources around you. Too many times teachers are hesitant to delegate. They become totally responsible for making something work, taking on not only all of the leg work but also all of the expense.

 ©1995 Teacher Created Materials, Inc.

Science Center (cont.)

Supplies

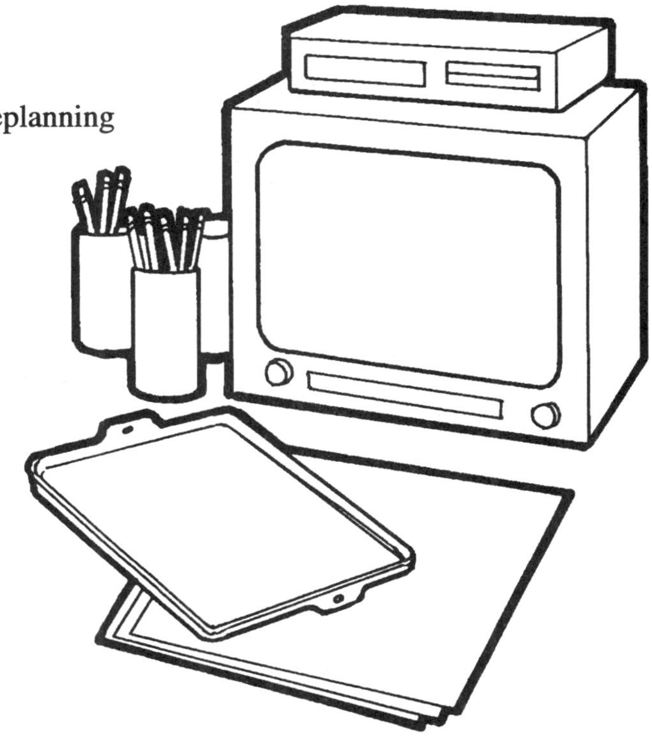

- large table
- smaller display table
- chairs
- five cookie sheets—more, if possible, for preplanning
- large closable plastic boxes
- bookshelves
- bulletin board space
- electrical outlet
- television
- VCR
- tape recorder
- blank tapes
- cleaning supplies, including paper towels
- construction paper
- crayons
- new pencils with erasers
- pencil cups
- one shirt-size gift box for each student (for a portfolio)

These are the most general of the supplies you will find useful. Remember that a list of materials needed for each activity is provided at the beginning of that activity's text as well as a picture of the stocked cookie sheet for the activity for teachers who prefer to see a picture of how it should look. By seeing what is needed, as well as reading a list, you will find it easier to set up your supplies for each activity quickly. (Additionally, the pictures will allow student helpers to assist you with the cookie sheet set-up, as you can simply say, "Make it look like this!")

Not Another Saturday!

This center will not take a whole Saturday to set up unless you want to become creative and play around with ideas as many teachers love to do. After compiling your materials, get an able-bodied helper to put everything in place in less than an hour or two. (See the center floor plan on page 22.)

Remember to Use It

Remember that even though it looks attractive and is a clever way to make your room look festive, the center is meant to remove as many organizational headaches from your day as possible. After each activity, have students replace what they have used. Get student helpers enrolled in cookie sheet set-up. We have also included a place for portfolios to be stored where they will be very accessible to your students. They can then take responsibility for the portfolios on whatever level you wish.

Floor Plan

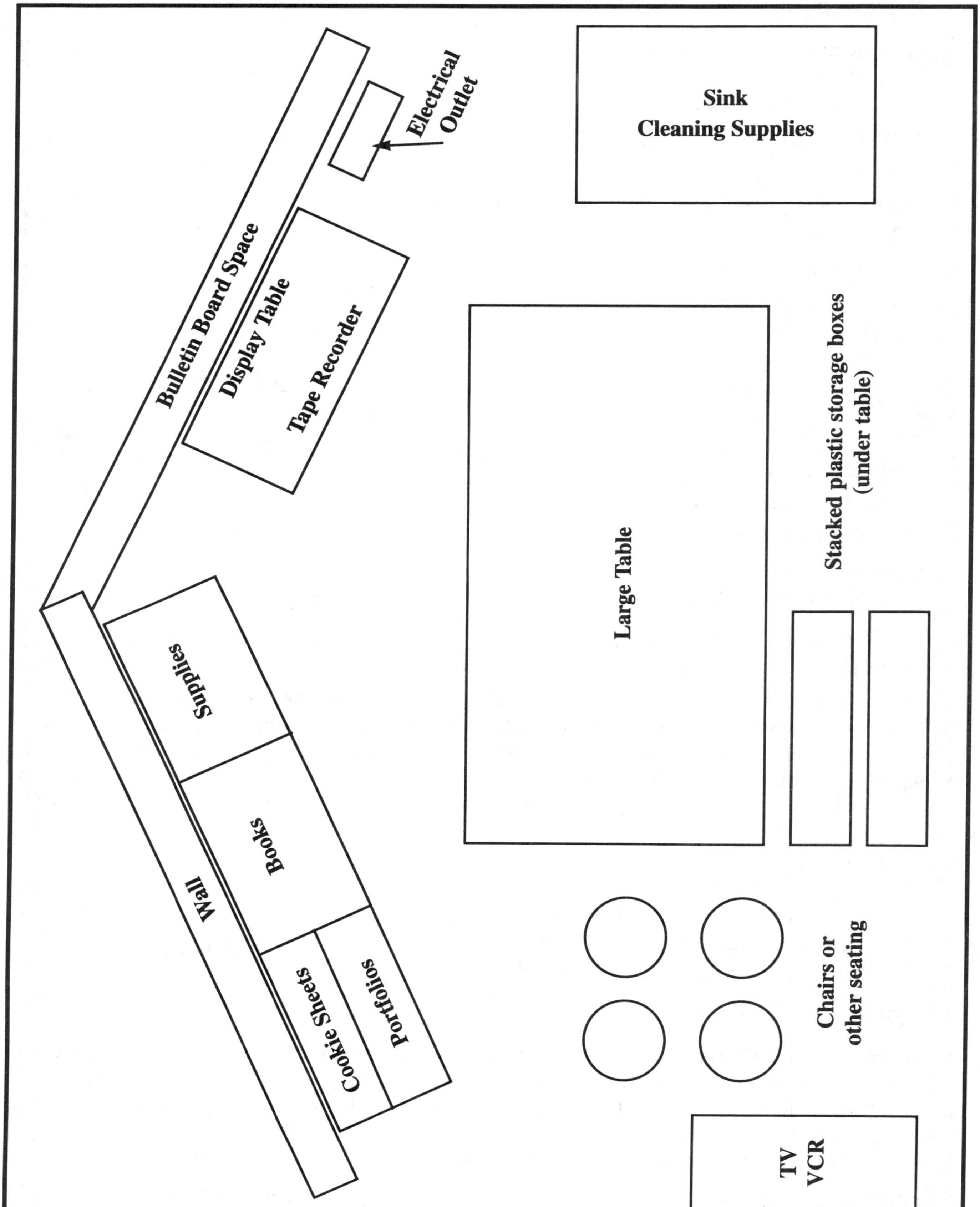

 ©1995 Teacher Created Materials, Inc.

Dear Parents,

We are busily setting up our Science Club Center and, in the interest of spending as little as possible of the money I have available for supplies, I am asking you to look around your home (and garage or storage area) for some of the items we need.

Here is the list I have put together:

- large table
- smaller display table
- chairs
- five cookie sheets—more, if possible
- large closable plastic boxes
- bookshelves
- science tapes for the VCR
- tape recorders
- blank cassette tapes
- cleaning supplies, including paper towels
- construction paper
- crayons
- new pencils with erasers
- pencil cups
- one shirt-size gift box for each student

We can also use indoor-outdoor thermometers, magnets, and plastic containers of all shapes and sizes.

If you have one or more of these items to spare, or if you could help pick up and deliver donations, please let me know. Any help will make our classroom more special. We plan to have an acknowledgement space on our bulletin board, recognizing your help and/or donations.

Thank you.

Sincerely,

____

- -

I can help! Please call me.

Name: ____

Student's Name: ____________________________________

Phone Number: _____________________________________

©1995 Teacher Created Materials, Inc.

Science Club Volunteers

We can use your help! Sign here if you would like to help our science clubs!

Name	Phone	Days and Times

 ©1995 Teacher Created Materials, Inc.

Official Science Club Membership Badges

Directions

Have students complete the information on the badges. Cut out the badges and prepare them for wearing by doing one of the following:

- Laminate and glue a safety pin to the back of the badge.
- Laminate, then attach a large paper clip to the badge and clip it to your clothing.
- Insert the badge in a plastic badge holder.

____

school

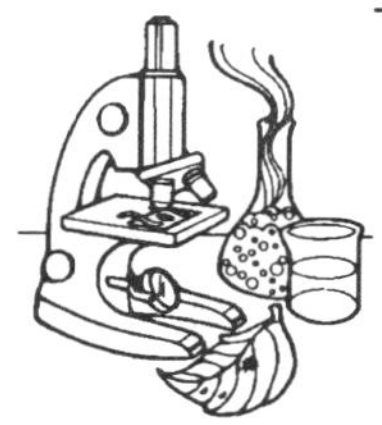

Official Scientist

____

student's name

____

group's name

____

school

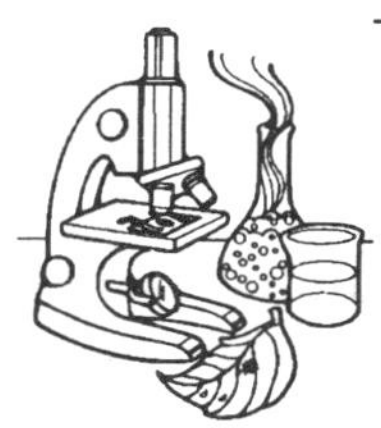

Official Scientist

____

student's name

____

group's name

____

school

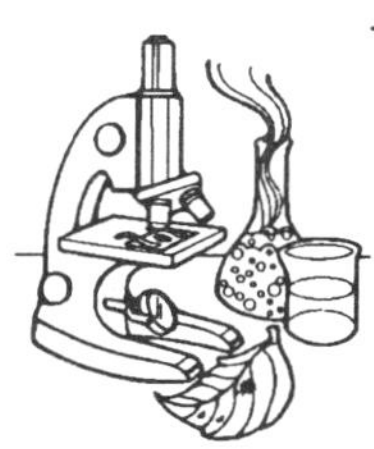

Official Scientist

____

student's name

____

group's name

Getting to Know Me

Purpose: to establish rapport and a sense of comfort among the members of a cooperative group

Skills: communication, oral language, decision making, and listening

Materials: one copy of pages 27 and 28 for each student, for each student, pencils or pens, and coloring materials

Procedures: As a class, go over the rules on "How We Work Together." These rules will let students know how to be effective members of a cooperative team. You can also enlarge the rules to poster size to display in the classroom.

Next, tell the children that they are going to get to know each other. Explain the simple information they will share by modeling the questions and answers on the "Getting to Know Me Game." (See the teacher script below.) Now, ask the students to sit in a circle in their cooperative groups. Give each student a copy of the page 27 activity sheet. Students will answer the questions about themselves and share their answers with their individual groups. If possible, have each group work with an older student helper or a parent volunteer to assist them in this activity.

To Simplify: Have pre-cooperative learners sit with their groups and have each think of his/her favorite food. Then, ask the students to listen to the favorite foods of each person in their group. Explain that a prize will go to the group whose members listen best and can tell what their "family's" favorite foods are. Offer the winning group something small like stickers or candy.

To Expand: Have advanced students share their "Getting to Know Me" pages and discuss their similarities and differences. Next, have them color their pages and make them into a book. Students may work together on a cover, thus creating their group's cover cooperatively.

Teacher Script: Today we are going to begin working in our groups. We are going to get to know each other. Before we start, let's go over our "How We Work Together" rules. *(Read the rules aloud.)* Let's talk about what these rules mean. *(Allow the children to discuss the rules.)* I think we are almost ready to start.

I need someone to play the "Getting to Know Me Game" with me. Okay, Amber will help me. Everyone, please look at your paper. There are five statements. The first one says, "My favorite color is." I will tell Amber my favorite color, and then I will let her tell me her favorite color. We will both take turns talking and listening to each other, and we will try to remember each other's favorite color. When we work in our groups, everyone will get a turn to tell the rest of the group about his or her favorite color, and so forth. (*Model the activity.*)

Now let's all sit in our groups and give it a try. Your helper will help you get started and answer your questions. I will walk around the room and help you, too.

Evaluation and Processing: You will be able to gauge each group's success easily by interacting with them during this activity. Process with your whole class by giving students a chance to share their group's answers.

 ©1995 Teacher Created Materials, Inc.

Name____

Getting to Know Me Game

Complete these statements. When everyone is finished, tell your family group your answers and listen to theirs.

1. My favorite color is ________________________________.
2. My favorite food is ________________________________.
3. I have __________ brothers and __________ sisters.
4. My favorite toy is ________________________________.
5. My favorite animal is ________________________________.

Use this space to draw a picture about some of your statements.

How We Work Together

1. When we work in groups, we always take turns.
2. We listen when other people talk.
3. Everyone in the group gets to have a turn.
4. If we cannot agree on something, we vote.
5. If we have a problem, we try to work it out. We do not fight.
6. If we do not know what to do, or if we have a question, we ask the group first and then the teacher.

 ©1995 Teacher Created Materials, Inc.

Observation Games—Memory

People

Purpose: To encourage students to master their own abilities to observe and remember details.

Skills: observation, memory, sequential and spatial thinking, communication and cooperation, oral and written language skills

Materials: one self-portrait "All About Me" (page 31) for each student, one copy of "All About Me" (page 31) enlarged for teacher use, one copy of "All About Me" group page (page 32) for each student, pencils with erasers for each student, student badges (page 25), a variety of art supplies such as crayons, construction paper, glue, paste, and scissors

Procedures: To begin this activity, talk with your whole class about the idea of memory and observation. Begin with this whole-class/volunteer demonstration:

> ***What Can We Remember?***
>
> Have a student volunteer stand before the class. Have the whole class take a long look at the student, asking the children to notice hair and eye color, what the student is wearing, etc. Next, have the volunteer stand outside the classroom and wait while the whole class remembers all they can about the person. Write and sketch on the board what the class remembers about the person. Next, have the volunteer student return and see how much the class remembered correctly and note the differences of opinion. Talk with your whole class about how important it is to be able to remember things to be a scientist. Discuss the idea that they can work to make their memories and observational powers better by practicing.

Next, have groups work together to play their own "What Can We Remember?" game. Have students work within their groups, with a partner, or in groups of three. Students should spend several minutes looking carefully at the faces of their partners and then, after one partner leaves the room, the other(s) should try to draw him/her from memory. Explain to the children that this is not about who can draw the best picture but who can remember the most about the person they are drawing.

Next, have each pair or group of three look at their drawings and see which parts they got right. Have them check the details with the "All About Me" sheet that each child has filled out beforehand (you may wish to have each child fill this out as part of the whole–classroom activity). Then have the groups talk about who made the drawing that had the most things right in it.

To Simplify: Use this activity as a partner activity rather than having students interact as cooperative groups to serve as a pre-cooperative learning readiness activity.

Observation Games—Memory

(cont.)

To Expand: Have children make their portraits of each other as detailed and artistic as possible, using a variety of art supplies to make them suitable for classroom display. Have a portrait gallery bulletin board to add color and fun to your classroom.

Teacher Script: Today we are going to talk about what it means to observe and what it means to remember. When we look carefully at something, we observe it. This is what scientists must do when they look at their experiments.

Now, let's try a little experiment of our own. Let's see how carefully we can observe and remember. Who would like to help? Can you help me, Bobby? Let's all observe, or take a very careful look at, Bobby. Here are the things we are looking for. *(Teacher refers to "All About Me," page 31. It is also possible to make this blackline master into poster size or into an overhead master to use during this part of the activity.)*

Let's take a good look at Bobby. While he stands outside *(Bobby goes out)*, let's try to think about all of the things we have here on our list. *(Teacher models the activity, asking students to contribute what they remember about Bobby, drawing a sketch of him on the board and listing the details as seen on "All About Me," page 31.)*

Now, let's have Bobby return and see what we got right! *(Teacher then has Bobby check his own description against that which the class made for him.)* That was great. We remembered a lot about Bobby. Now we are going to move into our cooperative Science Club groups and do this activity together. Everyone should get a partner, or you may work in a group of three people. Sit with your partners and decide who will be the first person to be "looked at." Take a good look and, after you have looked for a minute or two, have your partner go stand outside. Then take your pencils and crayons and make a picture of what you remember. Use your activity sheet to help you. (Have students use page 32 for illustrations.) When you are finished, have your partner come back in and look at what you have drawn. See how many things you got right about your partner. When all the partners have had a turn, let the rest of your group look at your pictures. After we are all done, we will all look at each other's pictures.

Evaluation and Processing: Have student groups come together as a whole group and share their pictures. Discuss with children the various outcomes they had and let them share their experiences. Have children work together to pin these pictures up on a bulletin board space. Restate that learning to remember things is just one of the ways one becomes a good scientist!

 ©1995 Teacher Created Materials, Inc.

All About Me

Group Name

Name ______________________________

My eyes are ______________________________.

My hair is ______________________________.

My skin is ______________________________.

I have ______________________________

______________________________.

I am wearing ______________________________

______________________________.

Here is a Picture of Me

All About Me *(cont.)*

Group Name ____

I am drawing ____

____.

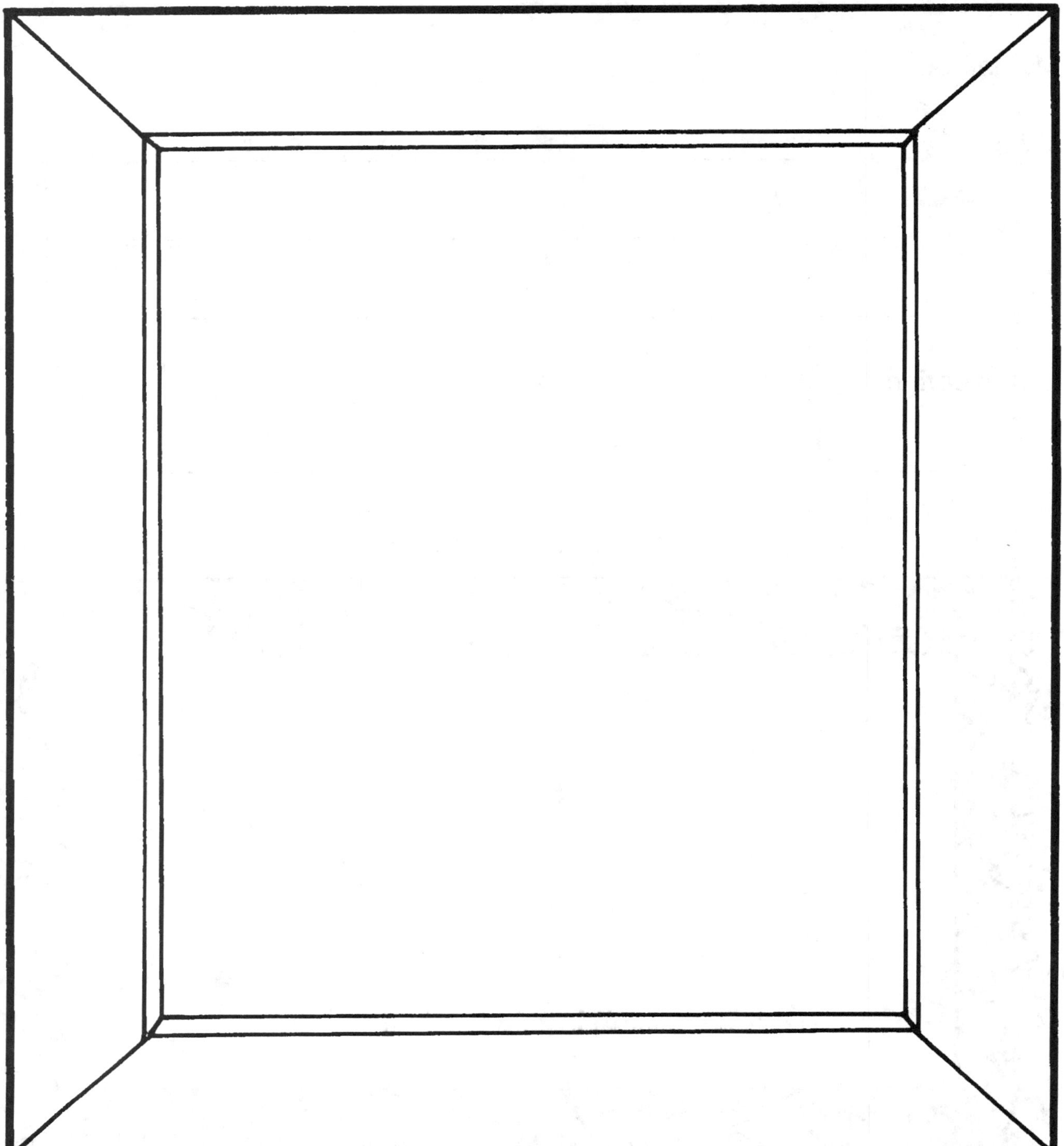

 ©1995 Teacher Created Materials, Inc.

All About Me Cookie Sheet

Observation Games—Nature Collections

Purpose: to encourage students to form the observational and organizational skills needed for the study of science

Skills: cooperation, oral and written language skills, sharing, and delegating

Materials: one small paper bag for each student, one copy of "Our Nature Collection" (page 36) for each group, one copy of "Nature Collection Labels" (page 37) for each group, pencils with erasers for each student, student badges (page 25), a variety of small collectible items from outdoors or common small classroom or home objects, tape or glue

Procedures: Students will work together to collect, compare, and label nature (or other) samples. Begin this activity with a whole-class discussion about all the wonderful things from nature that are right outside the door. Ask children to imagine as many things as possible that they think they will be able to collect. Then list these items on the board for them to refer to later in their cooperative groups. (Remember to tell children that when they make a nature collection they should not take living or dead animals, etc. You will know what parameters you should set with your particular group.)

Some of the things from nature that your group might list are:

- leaves
- seeds
- nuts
- berries
- twigs
- pebbles
- rocks

Have your students move into their cooperative Science Club groups and distribute a cookie tray with materials to each group. Explain to them that they should each first take a small brown bag and collect items outside with their group. (You may wish to have all the groups go together or go as single groups with parent volunteers or aides.) Next, they should use their materials to make their own classroom nature display. You will want to facilitate this activity, lending support to groups and also perhaps making this activity one where parent volunteers take part. After students have created their own displays and labeled the items, have each group share and explain their own display to the whole class.

 ©1995 Teacher Created Materials, Inc.

Observation Games—Nature Collections

To Simplify: Gather a variety of natural materials and place them in a bag on the cookie sheet for each group. Students will then move immediately to labeling and displaying their nature samples without the outside gathering step.

To Expand: Have children work with a parent volunteer to try to find the names of the leaves or flowers they have collected. Or, have children work on specific nature displays; e.g., rocks or flowers or leaves. Have children mount these on large pieces of construction or cardboard poster paper that can later be added to a classroom nature scrapbook.

Teacher Script: Today we are going to make our own nature displays! We can share and display them in our classroom. Let's think about and talk about all the wonderful things we can collect from nature that will fit in a paper bag this size. *(Teacher models the paper bag and begins a classroom discussion, listing ideas on the board for the class to refer to while in their cooperative groups.)*

We have listed a lot of things we think we can find on our playground for our displays. Now we will all take our paper bags and go to the playground to collect our nature samples. After we are all finished, we will sort through them and mount and label them. Let's go!

Evaluation and Processing: Have the team spokespersons show the groups' nature displays and place all of the displays in an area of the classroom for children to look at and comment on. Reinforce the ideas of labeling and organizing and why it is useful for scientists to have these skills.

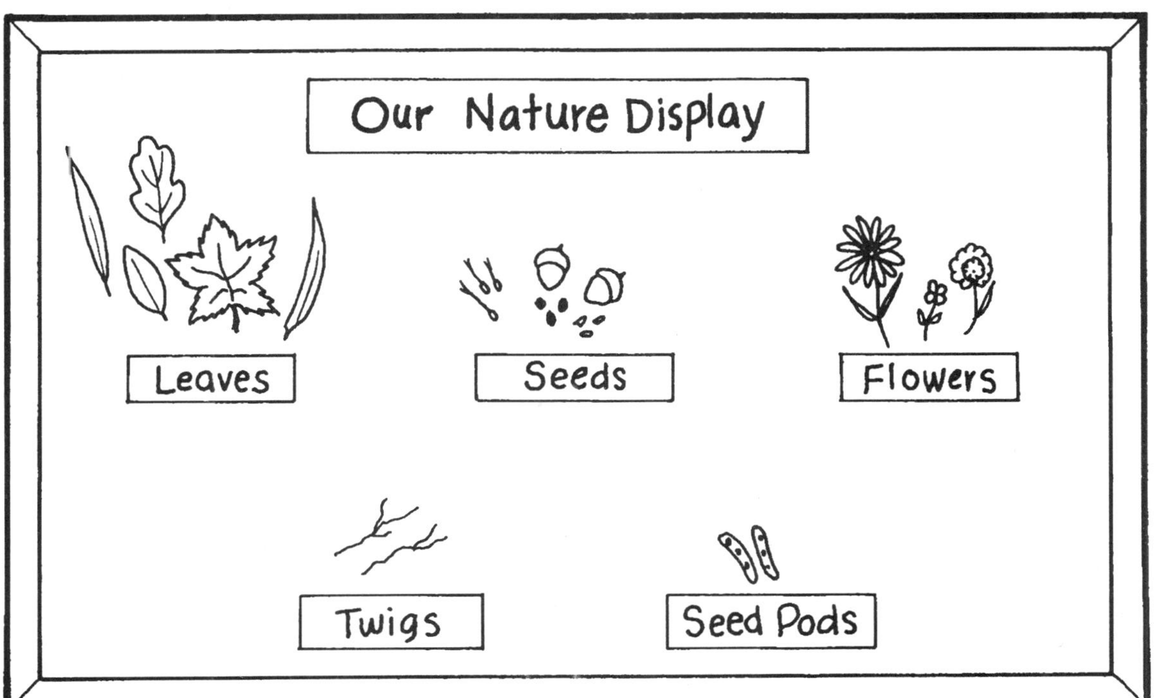

Our Nature Collection

Group Name ______________________________

How many of these did each group member collect?

Name	Leaf	Seed	Twig	Rock	Flower

 ©1995 Teacher Created Materials, Inc.

Nature Collection Labels

Use these labels to label your group nature displays. Use the blank boxes for other labels you may need that are not listed here.

Leaves	**Leaves**
Twigs	**Twigs**
Flowers	**Flowers**
Seeds	**Seeds**
Pebbles	**Pebbles**
Rocks	**Rocks**

©1995 Teacher Created Materials, Inc.

Nature Collection Cookie Sheet

 ©1995 Teacher Created Materials, Inc.

Charts

Purpose: to give students hands-on experience at making charts as they relate to scientific discovery

Skills: organization and evaluation of data, cooperation and thinking skills, sequential order, and reading charts and graphs

Materials: chart masters on pages 41 and 42, natural materials

Procedures: In this activity, students will sort natural items using charts as organizational tools. Begin this activity by discussing how important it is for scientists to have ways to keep track of the things they are studying. It is important to be organized. Talk about how organization and record keeping affects their daily lives and ask children to think of ways they keep track of things.

You might use examples around your room or talk about how you keep all the pieces of a puzzle in one box and count the pieces so that you know how many there are, etc. Then, after this discussion, talk with children about how they are going to sort and chart their own nature samples.

Model the activity, showing children how to use their charts by actually completing the investigation once as a whole class. Then, have each group take their cookie sheet full of supplies to their own Science Club area. Have each group work together to make their own simple chart. (Remember to save these charts as they will be used in the next activity on pages 46–48.) You may wish to use older students, parent volunteers, or aides to make this cooperative investigation go more smoothly.

(**Note**: There is another type of chart in Nature Collections on page 36. These two different types of charts will give children a chance to use thinking skills to figure out how to master a variety of different ways to record information, rather than setting a standard chart idea throughout the book. This will encourage children to think rather than simply memorize.)

To Simplify: To simplify this activity, have all the items that are to be sorted uniform and consistent for each group.

©1995 Teacher Created Materials, Inc.

Charts *(cont.)*

To Expand: Sort different kinds of samples. Have students make a chart for natural and man-made items, or have them sort shells and then rocks. This can be done again and again for practice, and students will enjoy it when they know exactly how to make a chart and a graph to once again practice the skill. Or combine this and "Making a Graph" on page 44 for more advanced students.

Teacher Script: Today we are going to learn to do another thing that scientists do so we can become better scientists in our own classroom. We are going to keep track of things using charts and graphs. Let's look at these examples of the chart and graph we will be using. Let's use them together now as a whole class so we can get the idea of what we are going to do in our Science Club groups.

Okay, this (*teacher holds up an enlarged example of chart master on page 41*) is an example of what a chart should look like. This side over here lists the things we want to keep track of. This bottom part is the part for people's names. Now, for this activity, we are using our nature samples. (Or use a variety of pre-sorted samples available to you inside your classroom. See suggested list on page 34). What is this first one over here? Right. The first item on number one is a leaf. The word "leaf" is written right here, but there is also a picture of it, so it's easy to understand. (The picture will make it possible for nonreaders to take part in this activity.) Now every member of your group will write his or her names on a line here, and then you will all work together to see how many leaves each one of you collected. On this example, the first name is Bobby. If we look here, we can see he has collected two leaves. So he wrote a two right here on this line so everyone in the group would know that Bobby has collected two leaves. Now let's look at the next person and see how many leaves it says that person collected...

(*Teacher models the entire chart form, getting feedback from whole class to ensure that they understand the concept thoroughly before they begin.*)

Let's all go to our cooperative groups and try this chart activity. I will walk around the room and help groups that need it. Let's go!

Evaluation and Processing: After groups have completed their charts, give each one an opportunity to have their spokesperson share about their chart and what it says. Let them have time to express how they liked the activity and how difficult or easy they felt this task was. Then have groups store their charts for the next activity, "Making A Graph".

 ©1995 Teacher Created Materials, Inc.

Chart Example

Group Name: *The Nature Ranger Club*

Item	Bobby	Rae	Maria	Jill	Shawndra
1  leaf	2	5	2	1	3
2 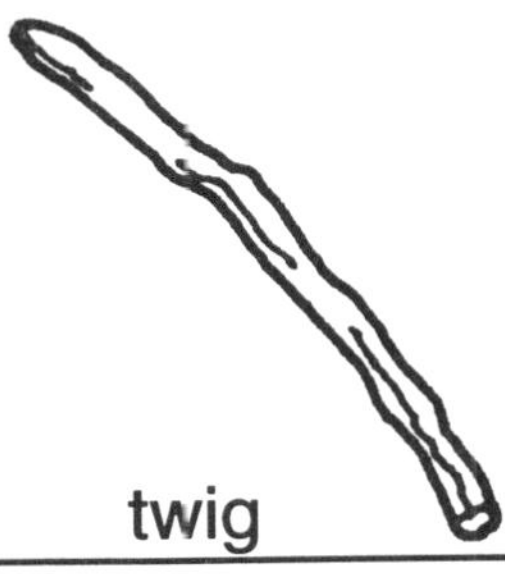 twig	0	4	0	4	1
3  flower	1	3	0	1	5
4  acorn	3	1	1	1	0
5  seed pod	5	0	6	1	2

Nature Chart

Group Name ____________________

1

______ ______ ______ ______ ______ ______

2

______ ______ ______ ______ ______ ______

3

______ ______ ______ ______ ______ ______

4

______ ______ ______ ______ ______ ______

5

______ ______ ______ ______ ______ ______

 ©1995 Teacher Created Materials, Inc.

Chart Cookie Sheet

Making a Graph

Purpose: to give students hands-on experience making graphs which illustrate scientific experiment or investigation outcomes, and for them to be able to transfer information from a chart to a graph

Skills: thinking, cooperating, reading charts and graphs, transferring information, organizing and sequencing skills, using mathematics

Materials: one copy of "Graph" enlarged (page 46) for teacher use, one copy of "Bar Graph Blank" (page 47) for each team, one copy of "Bar Graph Adding Page" (page 48) for each team, crayons or colored pencils, a ruler for each team, completed "Nature Chart" activity (page 42)

Procedures: In this activity, students will work together to create a bar graph using information they gathered in chart form on their "Nature Charts," page 42. To begin this activity, hold a whole-class discussion reminding students about the charts they made. Use the chart example master on page 41 to review the procedure students used when completing their team charts. (The chart and the graph masters relate to each other to make the modeling process work efficiently.)

Go through each step of making their team bar graph with them in a whole-class situation and list the steps on the board for them to refer to in their cooperative groups, as follows:

1. Look carefully at your team's chart.
2. Draw, in the boxes of the adding page, each of the things on your chart.
3. Make an addition problem for each of the things.
4. Write the names on the bar graph of each of the things on the chart.
5. Find the right number for each of the things and draw a line.
6. Make a bar.
7. Color the bar for each of the things.

Next, have children move into their cooperative groups to complete the graph, using the information from their already completed charts. You will want to be available to them to facilitate this process or have parent volunteers or older student helpers available to work with individual groups. After children have completed their graphs, have them compare their charts to their graphs and double-check their information.

To Simplify: Break this activity into two smaller parts. Have cooperative groups work together during one group meeting time to add their totals from page 48 and then make another activity of putting the information from page 48 on the Bar Graph Chart.

 ©1995 Teacher Created Materials, Inc.

Making a Graph *(cont.)*

To Expand: Have student groups work together, making a variety of bar graphs depicting different things. You can use the bar graph and chart forms for anything. They are made to be reusable in any context you would like to explore with your students.

Teacher Script: Today we are going to have more fun organizing our scientific information. First, let's all sit in our cooperative groups and look at the charts we made the other day. We are going to use these charts to make a bar graph. Let's look at these examples. Okay, here is an example we looked at the other day before we made our charts. Remember how we counted how many nature samples each one of us had collected and wrote the numbers down like this? Great. Now what we are going to do is make a graph. A graph will give us a picture of what we have written here.

Let's all take a look at this example bar graph (page 46). Why do you think we call it a bar graph? That's right. These are long bars. Let's look at this example more carefully. The first bar has the word "leaves" at the bottom of it. This means that it shows how many leaves this group had when they counted them all together. Let's all look at the number at the top of this bar. Can anyone tell me what that says? That is right. It says "thirteen" at the very top of this bar. That means they had thirteen leaves all together in their group. Now let's look at all the other bars and see what they mean. *(Teacher models the rest of the bar graph.)*

How do you think they looked at this chart and figured out how many leaves they had all together? What did they do? They added the leaves. Let's add the leaves on their chart and see if they did it right. *(Teacher models this process using "Bar Graph Adding Page.")* Now we are all going to use this adding activity page to add up the things on our charts so that we can make our own bar graphs. What we will really be doing is five addition problems like we do when we do math every day. Scientists use math every day. That's why it's so much fun to see how math and science work together! Okay, let's all work together to complete our adding forms and then, after we are done, we will work together to put this information on our bar graphs.

Evaluation and Processing: After children have completed the first step of the process, the addition activity page, you may want to stop and have an evaluation and processing of this part of the activity before you go on. After children have completed their bar graphs, let each group share about their own and have a chance to compare them to the other groups' charts, activity pages, and graphs.

©1995 Teacher Created Materials, Inc.

Graph

Group Name: *Nature Ranger Club*

	Leaves	Twigs	Flowers	Acorns	Seed Pods
30					
29					
28					
27					
26					
25					
24					
23					
22					
21					
20					
19					
18					
17					
16					
15					
14					
13					
12					
11					
10					
9					
8					
7					
6					
5					
4					
3					
2					
1					
0					

 ©1995 Teacher Created Materials, Inc.

Bar Graph

Group Name: ______________________________

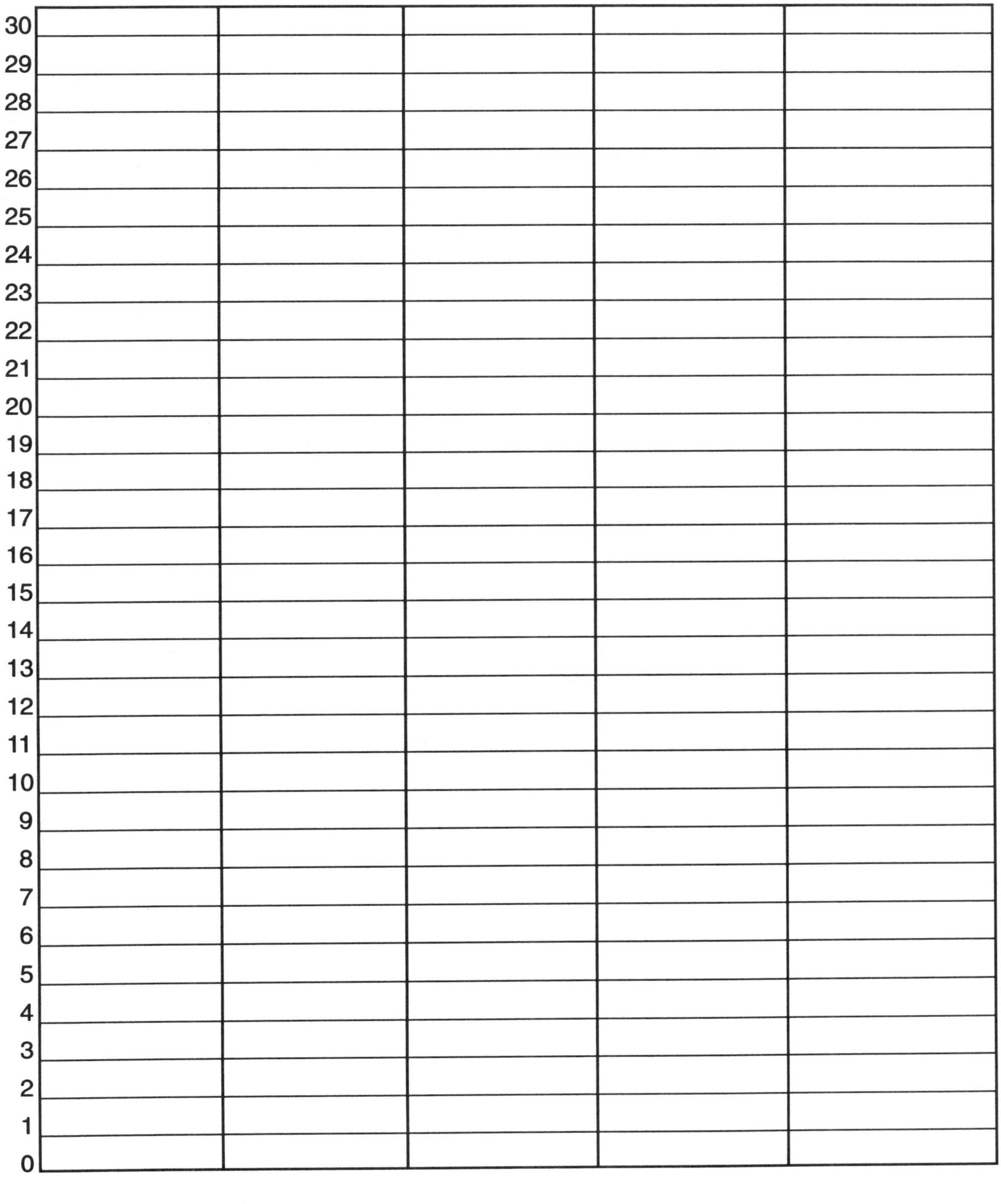

Bar Graph Adding Page

Group Name ______________________________

1	2	3	4	5
+ ______	+ ______	+ ______	+ ______	+ ______
+ ______	+ ______	+ ______	+ ______	+ ______
+ ______	+ ______	+ ______	+ ______	+ ______
+ ______	+ ______	+ ______	+ ______	+ ______
+ ______	+ ______	+ ______	+ ______	+ ______
= ______	= ______	= ______	= ______	= ______

 ©1995 Teacher Created Materials, Inc.

Bar Graph Cookie Sheet

Measuring Time

Purpose: to learn to measure time in seconds and minutes, and to apply that skill to scientific investigations and discovery

Skills: thinking, cooperation, evaluating information, reading minute and second hands, taking turns, and sharing equipment

Materials: one copy of "Measuring Time" activity (page 53) for each group, one jump rope and one bouncing ball for each group, pencils

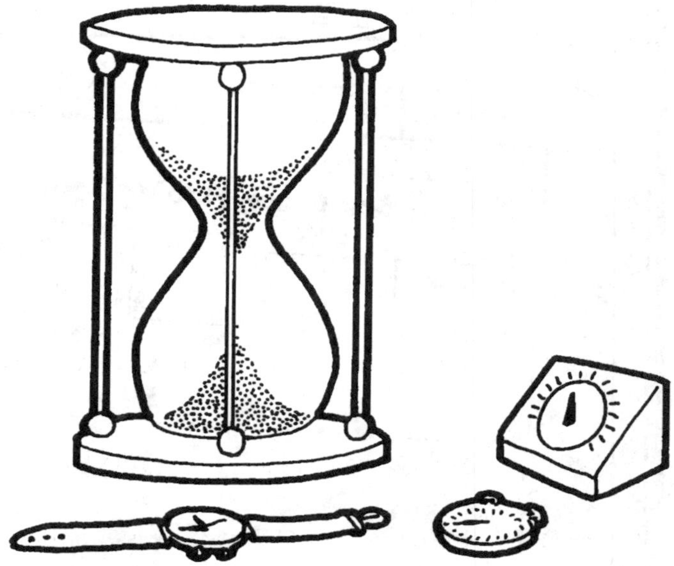

Procedures: In this activity, children will time various simple activities and keep records of the seconds and minutes used for each student to complete the activities. For this activity, each group will need a clock to measure minutes and seconds. A classroom clock that measures both is definitely acceptable, as is a wrist watch. Anything with a second hand will do. Naturally, you will want to have one clock for each group if they are small or hard to read. However, a large wall-mounted classroom clock should work well for everyone to use.

Begin this activity by modeling the process of measuring minutes and seconds in a whole-class demonstration. Model the activity using student volunteers. Explain to students that often scientific experiments are timed, and they will be learning to time themselves so that later they can use this skill in their group's scientific experiments. After the whole-class demonstration, have each group take their cookie sheet full of supplies and move to their group area. (Remember that this activity is very noisy, as are many cooperative activities, and that is part of the fun.)

Have cooperative groups work together to complete the activity and use the group worksheet to record their progress. Meet as a whole group to review the results. Give the children who could keep going the longest at the given activity in each group a chance to have a jump-off or bounce-off to see who can jump rope or bounce a ball the longest.

To Simplify: Have the students complete only one timed task, either jumping rope or bouncing a ball, but not both.

 ©1995 Teacher Created Materials, Inc.

Measuring Time *(cont.)*

To Expand: Have student groups think of other activities and measure the time it takes to do them. You may wish to use these activities to create a classroom olympics. Keep track of events and times on a large scoreboard.

Teacher Script: Today we are going to learn how to measure time in minutes and seconds in a really exciting way. To show you what we are going to do, I will need two students to help me. I need someone who knows how to jump rope and someone who can bounce this ball. Great. Now I am going to time Shawndra while she jumps rope. *(Teacher models activity, timing the student in minutes and seconds while she jumps rope and then entering the time on the master "Measuring Time" activity page. Then he/she does the same for the student bouncing the ball.)*

Now, we are all going to work together in our cooperative groups, taking turns jumping rope and bouncing the ball to see how many seconds and minutes we can do these things. You will have to decide who will go first, who will watch the clock, and who will record the time. Work together and if you need help, I will be here to answer questions and see how you are doing. Okay, team leaders, come and get the cookie sheet for your group and let's start timing!

Evaluation and Processing: End this activity by having children come together to discuss their results. Have the person from each group that either jumped rope or bounced the ball the longest, try again with the other "winners" from each group. See who ends up doing it the longest. Award "Way to Go" ribbons (page 52) to everyone or just to the winners, depending on your preference. Post the names of winners (and all other students, if you wish) with their record times on a classroom wall.

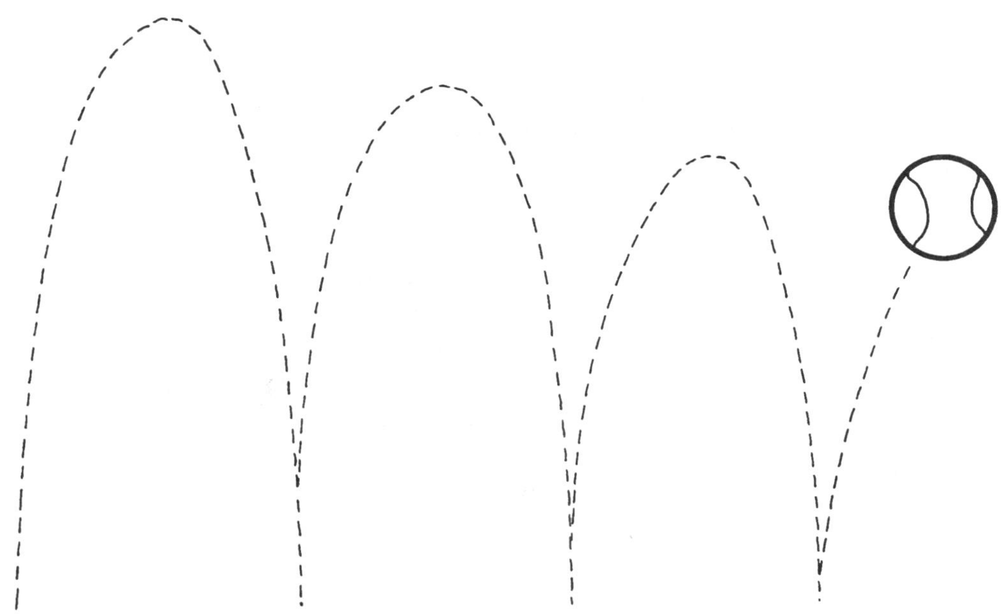

Winner Awards

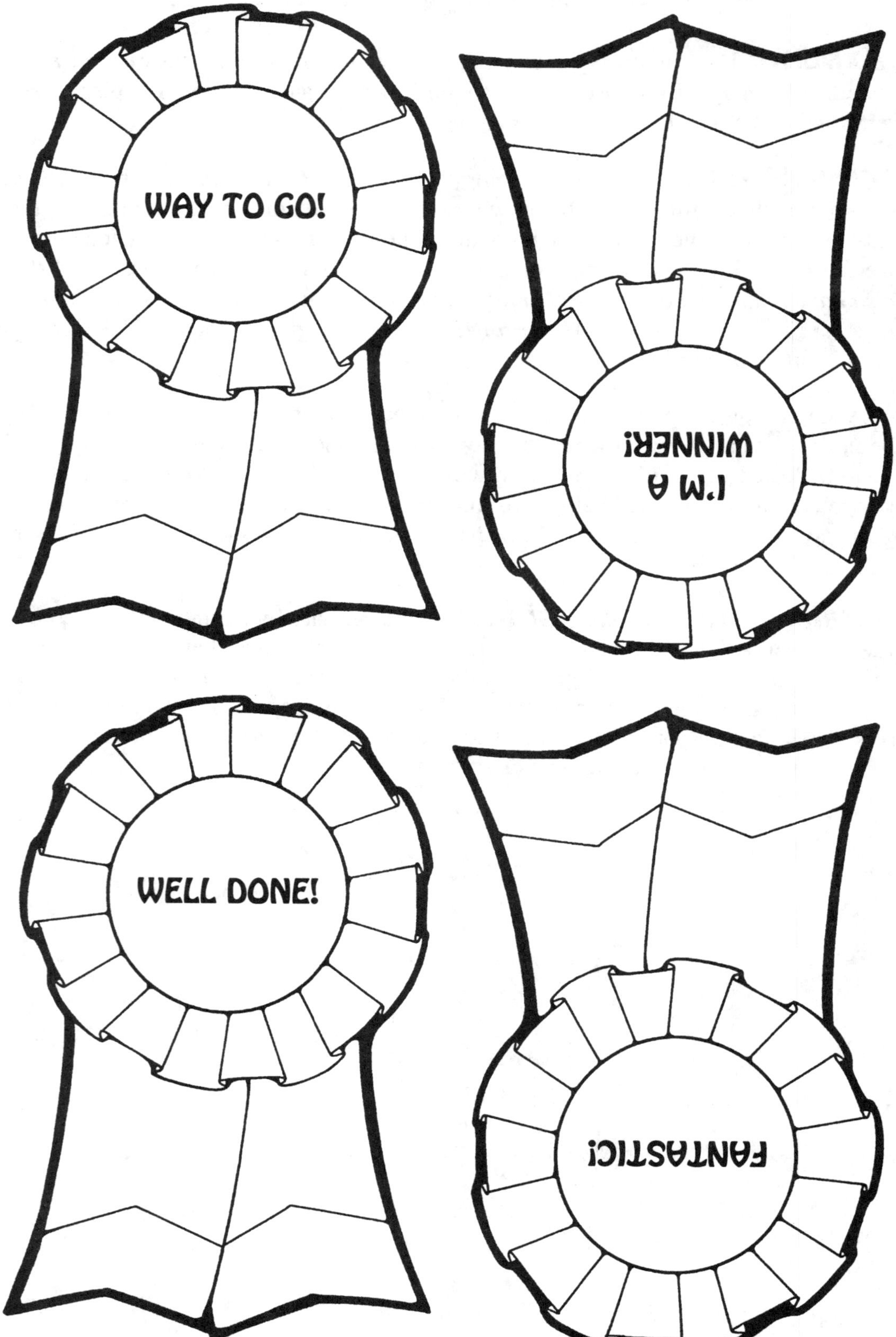

 ©1995 Teacher Created Materials, Inc.

Measuring Time

Group Name

____

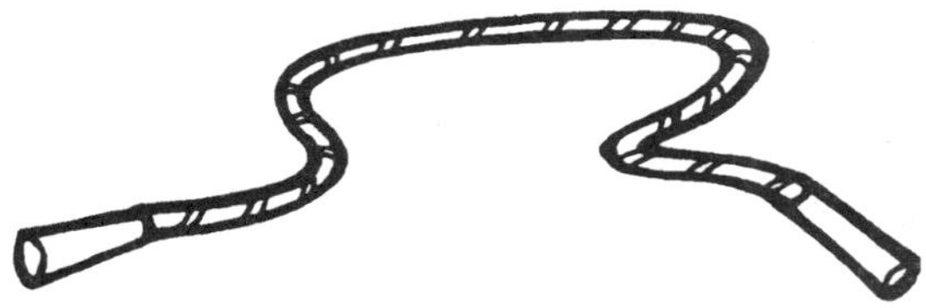

Name	Jumping Rope	Bouncing Ball
______________________	Minutes ____________ Seconds ____________	Minutes ____________ Seconds ____________
______________________	Minutes ____________ Seconds ____________	Minutes ____________ Seconds ____________
______________________	Minutes ____________ Seconds ____________	Minutes ____________ Seconds ____________
______________________	Minutes ____________ Seconds ____________	Minutes ____________ Seconds ____________
______________________	Minutes ____________ Seconds ____________	Minutes ____________ Seconds ____________

©1995 Teacher Created Materials, Inc.

Measuring Time Cookie Sheet

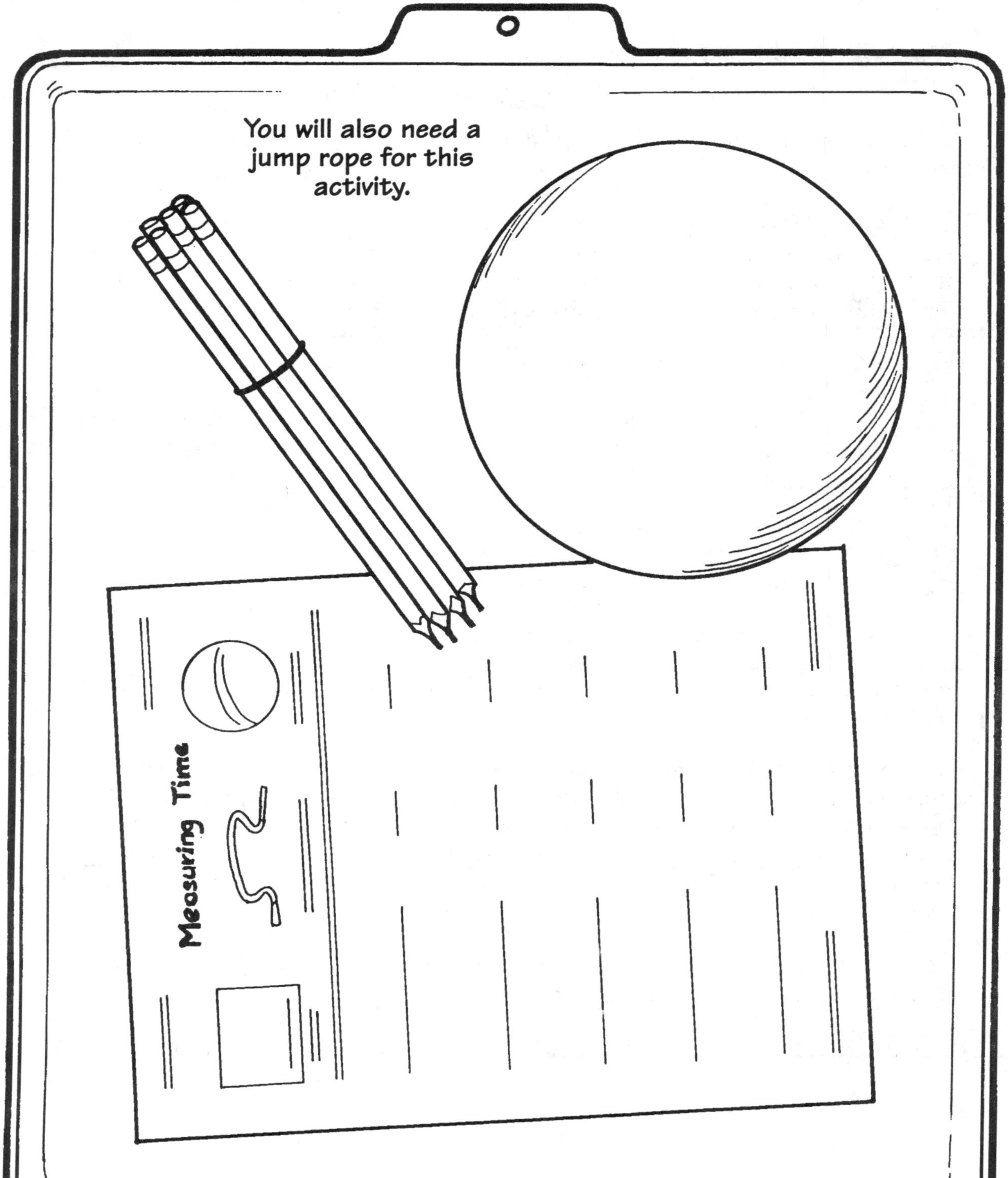

 ©1995 Teacher Created Materials, Inc.

Measuring Liquids

Purpose: to learn to measure liquids in standard American and international forms of measurement and later apply to scientific investigation and discovery

Skills: thinking, cooperation, guessing and checking (estimating and verifying), and using measuring tools

Materials: for each group—one copy of liquid measurement "Guess and Check" activity (page 57), one measuring teaspoon, one measuring tablespoon, one 8-ounce measuring cup, clean milk cartons in pint, quart, and half-gallon sizes, clean plastic soda (pop) bottles in one and two liter sizes, one large bowl, pitcher, or other container (for water supply)

Procedures: Students will work together to see the relationship between a variety of measurements and will also be able to measure liquids in a variety of different ways using standard measures. To begin this activity, talk about the various reasons why people need to measure things. Discuss the reasons a scientist might need to measure something. Here are a few ideas to get you started:

1. A chemist measures liquid chemicals.
2. A pharmacist measures the ingredients in medicine.
3. A botanist measures how much water to give plants.

Have a whole-class discussion about the ways that liquid measurement can be useful in everyday activities (such as cooking) as well as for scientists.

Next, explain to students that they will be conducting a few scientific investigations in their cooperative groups. Display the measuring tools and model one activity from the "Guess and Check" activity page to the whole class before students move to their cooperative groups. Make sure students understand the process of guessing and checking. After groups have completed this activity and filled out their worksheets, meet again as a whole class to let students talk about their investigations and what they have discovered.

To Simplify: Provide students with a smaller array of measuring tools and have them fill out only part of the activity page.

To Expand: Have students bring containers from home or look for containers in the classroom to fill with liquid for further liquid measurement investigation.

Measuring Liquids *(cont.)*

Teacher Script: Today we will be learning another important skill that we will use a lot as scientists. We are going to learn about liquid measurement. Can anyone tell me what liquid means?

Let's list some of the liquids we know about. *(Teacher conducts whole-class discussion and lists the liquids on the board.)* How can we tell if something is a liquid? Let's talk about some of the things a liquid can do.

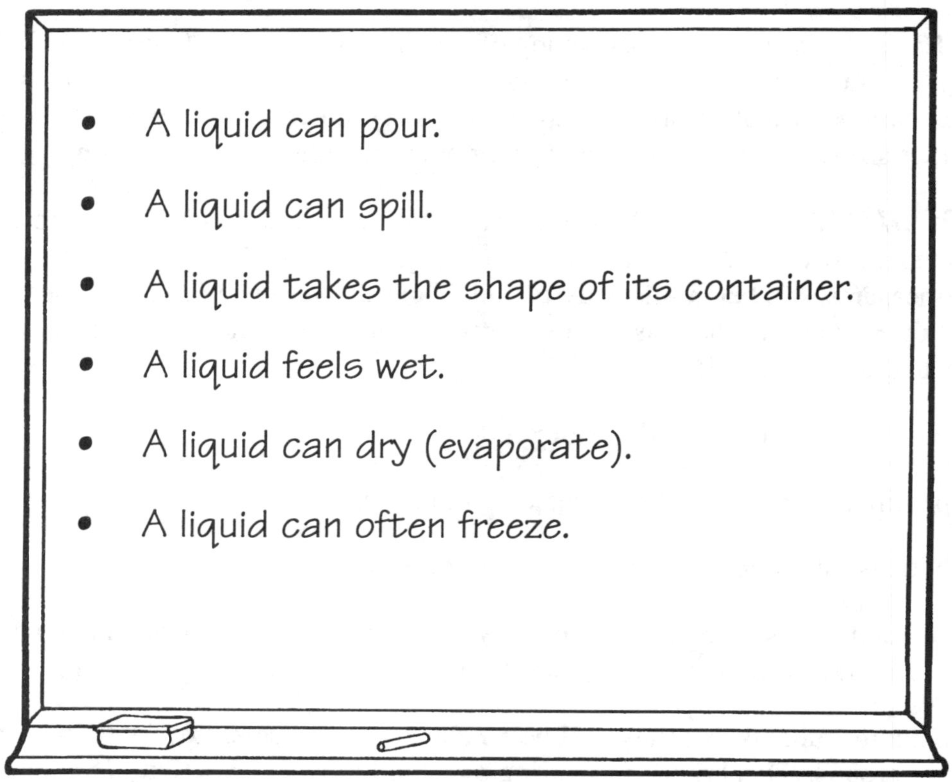

Water is an easy liquid to use for an investigation. My large pitcher is full of water. These are my measuring tools. *(Teacher displays and names measuring tools.)* The investigation we will do has two parts: guessing and checking. Your activity page has spaces for recording both of these steps. I will show you how to complete one of the questions. *(Teacher models guessing and checking and fills in the correct spaces on a sample activity page.)*

Take turns guessing and recording data in your groups. The team leaders may take their cookie sheets to their groups and fill up the large containers with water. I will walk around the room and help. (This would be a good time to enlist the help of older student helpers or parent volunteers.)

Evaluation and Processing: When all groups have finished their investigations and recorded their findings, have students come together to compare their results. Encourage students to discuss whether or not their guesses were always correct. Were they surprised by any of their findings?

 ©1995 Teacher Created Materials, Inc.

Guess and Check

Group:________________________

	Guess	**Check**
How many teaspoons are in a cup?	________	________
How many tablespoons are in a cup?	________	________
How many cups are in a pint?	________	________
How many cups are in a quart?	________	________
How many cups are in a half-gallon?	________	________
How many pints are in a quart?	________	________
How many pints are in a half-gallon?	________	________
How many quarts are in a half-gallon?	________	________
Which is bigger, a pint or a liter?	________	________
Which is bigger, a quart or a liter?	________	________
Which is bigger, a quart or two liters?	________	________
Which is bigger, a half-gallon or two liters?	________	________

Measuring Liquid Cookie Sheet

Linear Measurement

Purpose: to learn how to use linear measurement so that these skills can later be applied to a variety of scientific and practical investigations

Skills: thinking, cooperation, guessing and checking (estimating and verifying), and using measuring tools

Materials: one linear measurement "Guess and Check" activity (page 62) for each team, one copy of "How Big is My Dinosaur? (page 63) for each team, one copy of "Measuring at Home" activity (page 64) for each child, one copy of "Parent Letter" (page 65) for each child, "Linear Measuring Tools Check-Out Sheet" (page 66), 1-foot rulers marked in inches, 5 or 6-foot tape measures marked in inches, yardsticks marked in inches and feet, paved playground space or a long roll of butcher paper and a place to unroll it, pencils and/or playground chalk, encyclopedias and/or other reference books containing facts about dinosaurs

Procedures: Students will work together to see the relationship between a variety of tools to measure the lengths of things and will measure the length of assorted objects. To begin this activity, talk about the various reasons why people need to measure things. Discuss the reasons a scientist might need to measure something. Here are a variety of ideas to get you started:

1. A scientist who studies physics measures changes in the lengths of things when they are heated and cooled.
2. A doctor measures children to see whether they are the right heights for their ages and weights.
3. A scientist who studies dinosaurs measures the bones he/she finds to figure out how tall and how long the dinosaur was when it was alive.

Have a whole-class discussion about the ways that linear measurement can be useful in everyday activities (such as building something) as well as for scientists. (**Note:** *If using the metric system, convert measurement-related activities accordingly.*)

> ***Guess and Check:*** Next, explain to students that they will be conducting a few scientific investigations in their cooperative groups. Display the measuring tools and remind students that they used the "Guess and Check" method when they investigated liquid measure. (Make sure students understand the process of guessing and checking. Model one or two guess and check measurements with items on your desk.) After groups have completed the guess and check activity pages, meet again as a whole class to discuss anything that needs attention before going on with the next activity, "How Big is My Dinosaur?"

Linear Measurement *(cont.)*

How Big is My Dinosaur?:

To begin this part of the activity, have students decide together in their cooperative groups on a dinosaur to use in building their measurement clues. When they have decided on the dinosaur, they should write its measurements on the "How Big is My Dinosaur?" activity sheet. If the measurements are in inches, the students should convert them to feet and vice versa. (Students may require help with the conversion step.) Then assign a Secret Dinosaur Number to each group. Each Science Club group should go out separately to the playground with an older student helper, parent volunteer, or aide and—using chalk and linear measurement tools—make lines to show the dimensions of their dinosaur. Before leaving the playground, each group should write its dinosaur number near the lines. (If no playground space is available to you, use long, rolled-out pieces of butcher paper. You will probably need to adapt the activity by using only height or length rather than both dimensions.)

When each group returns to the classroom, they should give their activity sheet to the teacher who will mix them up and hand them out again, making sure that no group gets its own clues.

All groups may then return to the playground and, by using their measuring tools, identify the dinosaur described on the activity sheet they received. Finally, meet as a whole group to check the results.

To Simplify: Have students complete only the "Guess and Check" activity sheet.

To Expand: Have students modify and repeat the "Dinosaur" activity by playing "How Big is My Mountain?" or "How Tall is My Skyscraper?"

Teacher Script: Today we will be learning another important skill that we will use a lot as scientists. We are going to learn about linear measurement. Can anyone tell me what linear means? That's right. It means length. What things do we want to know the length of? Let's talk about them. (Class discussion of measuring length.)

Guess and Check: First, we are going to work together to practice using linear measuring tools. Here are the tools we will be using: a 1-foot ruler marked in inches, a measuring tape marked in feet and inches, and a yardstick marked in feet and inches. We will be using the same guess-and-check method that we used for liquid measurement. I will do one for you. I think this book is about 1 foot tall and 8 inches across so I will write that guess on the board. Now I will check with my tape measure and write the actual measurement next to my guess. We will work in our Science Club groups to fill out the "Guess and Check" activity sheet and then we will compare the results all together. Let's start!

 ©1995 Teacher Created Materials, Inc.

Linear Measurement *(cont.)*

Measuring Dinosaurs:

To begin this part of the activity each group will decide on a dinosaur and find secret measurement clues by looking in reference books. You will write your clues on this clue sheet. (Display "How Big is My Dinosaur?," page 63.) While you are waiting for your turn to go out to the playground, you may work together to change your measurement clues from feet to inches or from inches to feet. Before you go to the playground, I will give each group a secret dinosaur number. When you get to the playground, you will use chalk and your linear measurement tools to make lines showing the size of your secret dinosaur. Then write your secret number near the lines you made. When you come back to the room, give your clue sheet to me.

When all groups are back from the playground, I will pass out the clue sheets. Check to make sure you do not get the one your group made.

Now we will all go back to the playground. Use your measuring tools to find the dinosaur described on the activity page your group received. Then we will meet as a whole group to check our results. Those who want to may take time to complete the bonus question.

Evaluation and Processing:

When all groups have finished their investigations and recorded their findings, have students come together to compare their results. Encourage students to discuss whether or not their guesses were always correct. Was it harder to make clues or to follow the directions and measure? Were they surprised by any of their findings?

Guess and Check

Group: ______________________________

Find an object to measure.
Guess its height or length. Then measure.
Guess its width. Then measure.
Record your guesses and measurements.

	Guess	**Check**
1. BOOK		
height or length	________	________
width	________	________
2. DOOR		
height or length	________	________
width	________	________
3. STUDENT DESK TOP		
height or length	________	________
width	________	________
4. TEACHER DESK TOP		
height or length	________	________
width	________	________
5. WINDOW		
height or length	________	________
width	________	________

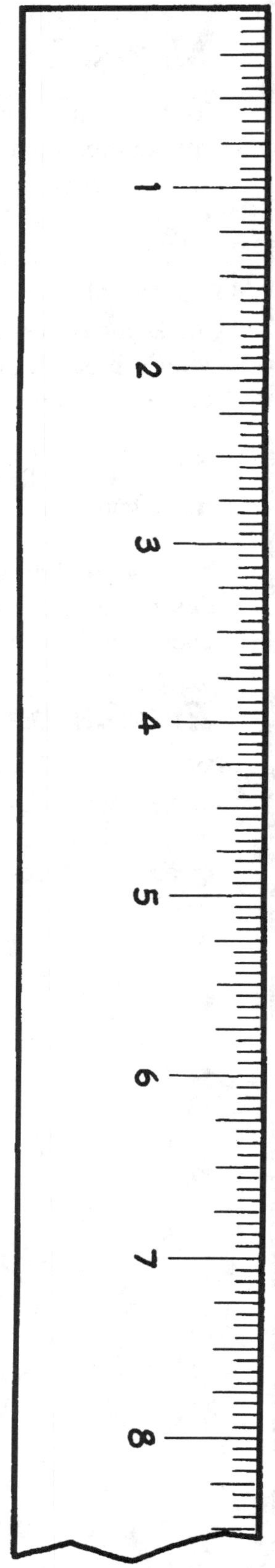

 ©1995 Teacher Created Materials, Inc.

How Big is My Dinosaur?

Group Identifying the Dinosaur ____

____

Instructions:

See if you can find the dinosaur that matches the description below by using your measuring tools to check its length and height on the playground.

Fill in the blanks at the bottom of the page.

Bonus:

Check in reference books to discover the name of the dinosaur being described.

____

Here is a description of this dinosaur:

Length in feet ____________________

Length in inches ____________________

Height in feet ____________________

Height in inches ____________________

____

This is the dinosaur number __________.

Its real name is ____________________.

Measuring at Home

Name: ____________________________________

Find an object to measure. Guess its height or length. Then measure. Guess its width. Then measure. (You may cut out and use the ruler on this page.) Record your guesses and measurements.

	Guess	Check
1. BED		
height or length	________	________
width	________	________
2. TABLE		
height or length	________	________
width	________	________
3. CHEST OF DRAWERS		
height or length	________	________
width	________	________
4. KITCHEN SINK		
height or length	________	________
width	________	________
5. REFRIGERATOR		
height or length	________	________
width	________	________

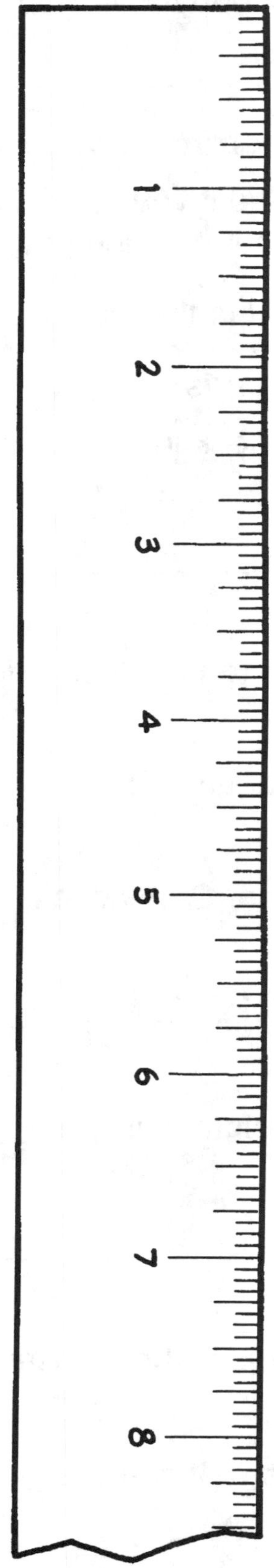

 ©1995 Teacher Created Materials, Inc.

Measuring at Home

Dear Parents,

As part of our current cooperative learning unit we are studying linear measurement. We are measuring the length, height, and width of things in inches, feet, and yards in the classroom. Please reinforce this learning experience by helping your child fill out the "Measuring at Home" activity sheet your child will be bringing home. He or she will also be bringing home a ruler, tape measure, and/or yardstick. Please help keep track of these tools and make sure they are returned to school. Also, ask your child to explain our guess-and-check method to you.

We will soon be doing an activity in school called "How Big is My Dinosaur?," and we could really use some parent helpers to make it run smoothly. If you would like to help, please fill in the slip at the bottom of this letter and return it to me.

Even if you can't help this time, please feel free to drop in anytime and watch the fun.

Sincerely,

____

I would like to help. Please call me.

Name: ____

Student's name: ____

Phone number: ____

Best time to call: ______________________________________

Linear Measuring Tools Check-Out Sheet

Science Club Group ______________________________

Name	Ruler	Measuring Tape	Yardstick

 ©1995 Teacher Created Materials, Inc.

Linear Measuring Cookie Sheet

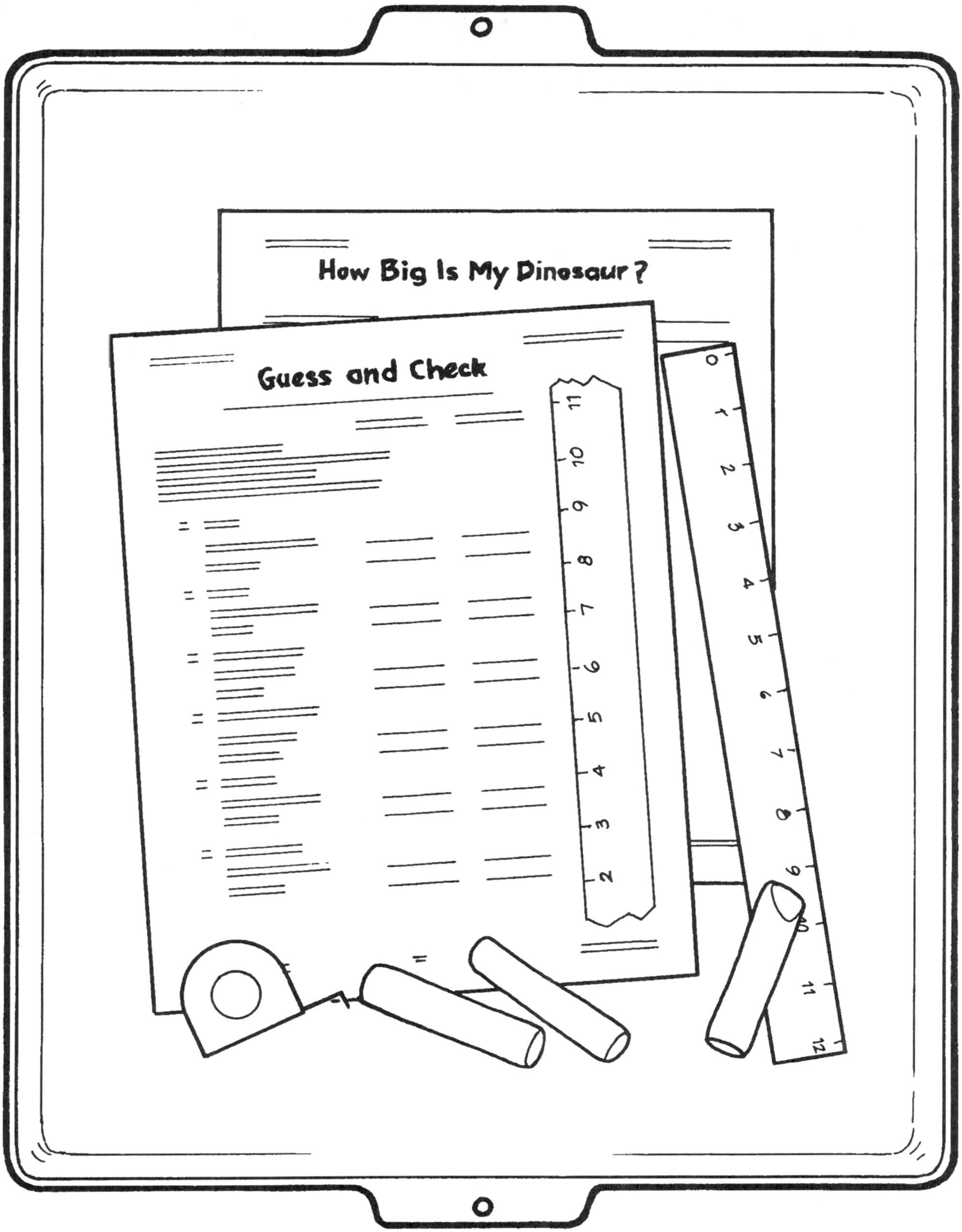

Reading a Thermometer—What's Hot and What's Not

Purpose: to provide students with practice in reading temperatures on thermometers

Skills: observing, recording data, drawing conclusions

Materials: sturdy indoor-outdoor thermometers (Fahrenheit and Celsius), warm water, cold water, clear plastic bowls for water, one copy of "Measuring Temperature" (page 69) for each child, colored pencils

Procedures: Students will have the opportunity in this activity to actually see the temperature on the thermometers go up and down with warmth and cold. Give them enough time in their groups so that everyone gets an opportunity to make this happen. Have them read the thermometer first at room temperature and then take turns putting it in warm and then in cold water. Call their attention to the fact that thermometers are marked off (calibrated) by two's. Although the activity page calls for reading a Fahrenheit thermometer, Celsius thermometers are also marked off by two's. Encourage discussion in the Science Club groups. (Why didn't everyone get the same temperatures? Why are thermometers marked off by two's? Etc.)

To Simplify: Give students some practice in reading thermometers prior to the activity.

To Expand: Have students explore the uses for Celsius thermometers. Why are they not generally used in the United States?

Teacher Script: Today you will all have the opportunity to make the temperature reading on a thermometer go up and down. When you get to your groups, look at all of the thermometers. Choose the Fahrenheit thermometer *(teacher displays a Fahrenheit thermometer)* that will be your "official" one and record its temperature on your activity page. This is called room temperature. It is simply the temperature of the air in this room right now.

Now take turns putting the thermometer in warm and cold water and reading and recording the temperature. Remember that thermometers are marked off in two's.

Evaluation and Processing:

Come back into a whole-class group to discuss how it felt to have a hands-on experience reading thermometers. Why are real experiences helpful?

 ©1995 Teacher Created Materials, Inc.

Measuring Temperature

Group Name ______________________________

Shade in the thermometer to show its actual appearance. On the lines below, write the temperatures it shows on the thermometers.

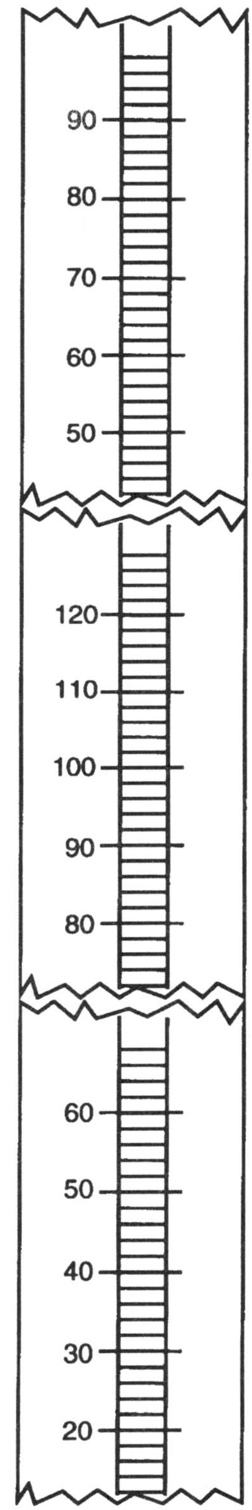

This is a picture of a section of our Fahrenheit thermometer at room temperature.

The temperature it shows is ________ ° F.

This is a picture of a section of our Fahrenheit thermometer after three minutes in warm water.

The temperature it shows is ________ ° F.

This is a picture of a section of our Fahrenheit thermometer after three minutes in very cold water.

The temperature it shows is ________ ° F.

Temperature Cookie Sheet

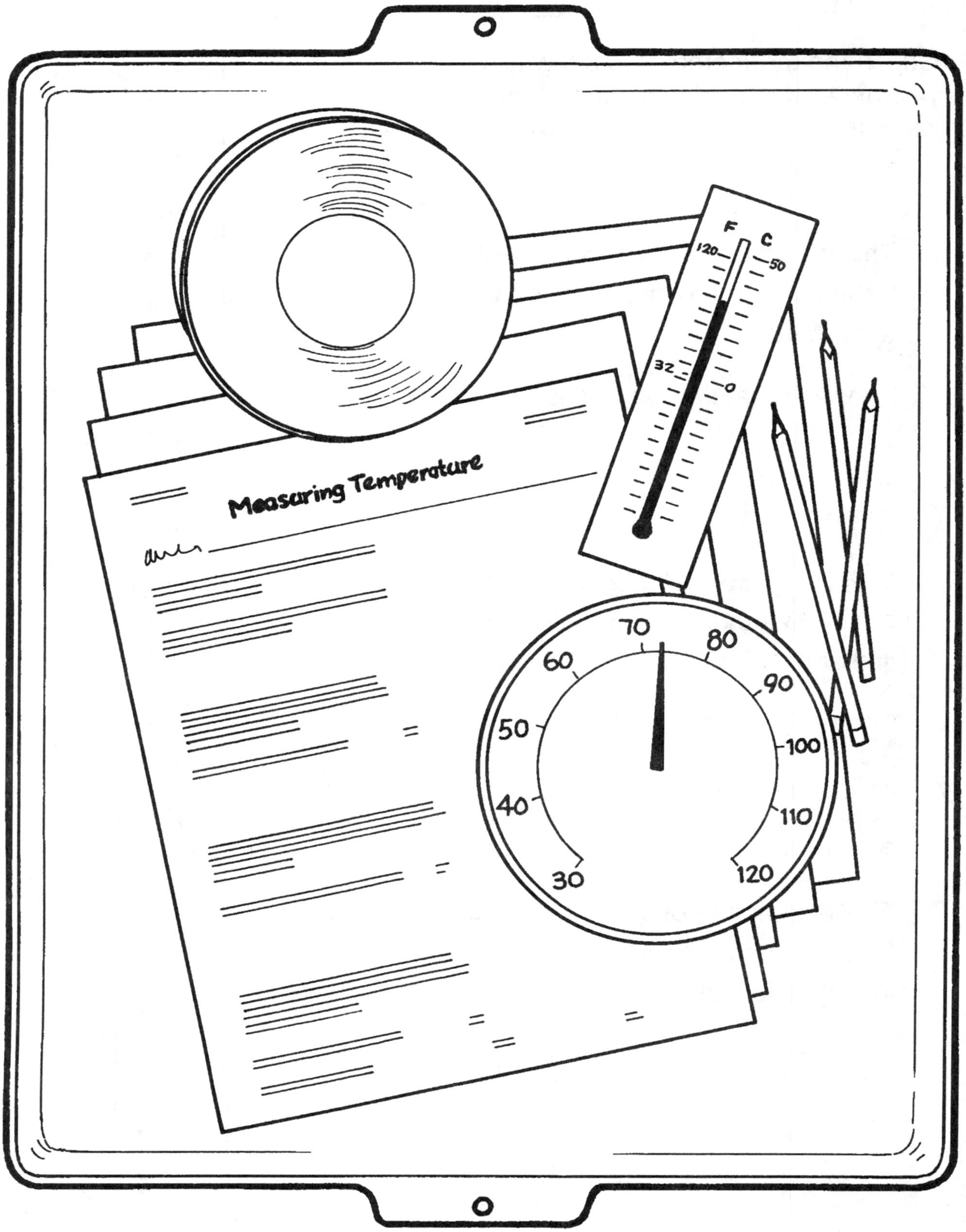

 ©1995 Teacher Created Materials, Inc.

Magnet Fun

Purpose: to provide an opportunity for students to predict which objects will be attracted to magnets and then check predictions by testing

Skills: predicting and verifying, classifying, sorting, collecting and organizing data, and reporting data

Materials: magnets, a collection of objects (pins, paper clips, coins, rubber bands, marbles, chalk, erasers, nails, costume jewelry, etc.), writing materials, one copy of Magnet "Guess and Check" activity (page 72) for each group

Procedures: In this activity, students will work in their Science Club groups, first discussing and predicting which objects are magnetic and then testing the objects with magnets. They should list the objects on their "Guess and Check" page, write "yes" for magnetic or "no" for not magnetic under "Guess", test the object with a magnet, and then write "yes" or "no" under "Check". Once they have completed their guess-and-check procedure, ask students to discuss the things that were magnetic. What do these things have in common?

(Caution students to keep all magnets away from computers and computer disks.)

To Simplify: Give students fewer objects to test.

To Expand: Have students check magnetism through paper, water, glass, etc., and draw conclusions about the effect of other materials on magnetism. Some students may be interested in exploring the reasons for keeping magnets away from computers and computer disks.

Teacher Script: Today we are going right to our cooperative groups with our cookie sheets full of materials. You will be discussing whether or not the objects on your cookie trays will be attracted to magnets. First, look at your activity page. List the names of the objects you will be testing. Talk about them in your groups. Guess whether or not each one will be magnetic and write down your guess—"yes" or "no". Then test each object with a magnet. Write down your results.

When we come back together in our large group, we will talk about what magnetic objects have in common. Talk about that in your group and be ready with some ideas.

Evaluation and Processing: Have students discuss any surprises they had. What did they learn from wrong guesses?

Guess and Check

Group: ______________________________

- List the objects you will be testing.
- Talk about them in your group and guess whether or not each one will be magnetic.
- Write down your guesses—yes or no.
- Test each object with a magnet.
- Write down your results—yes or no.

Object	Guess	Check
1.		
2.		
3.		
4.		
5.		
6.		
7.		
8.		
9.		
10.		

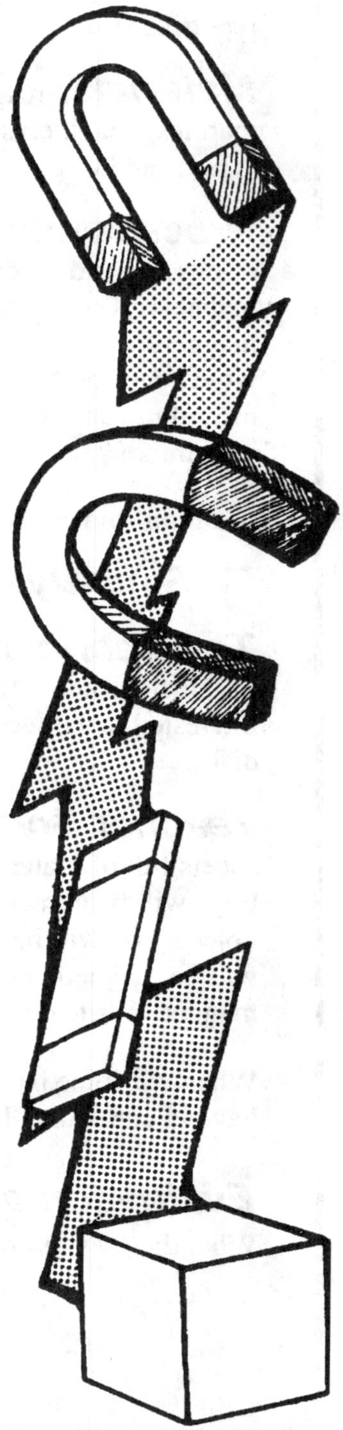

 ©1995 Teacher Created Materials, Inc.

Magnet Fun Cookie Sheet

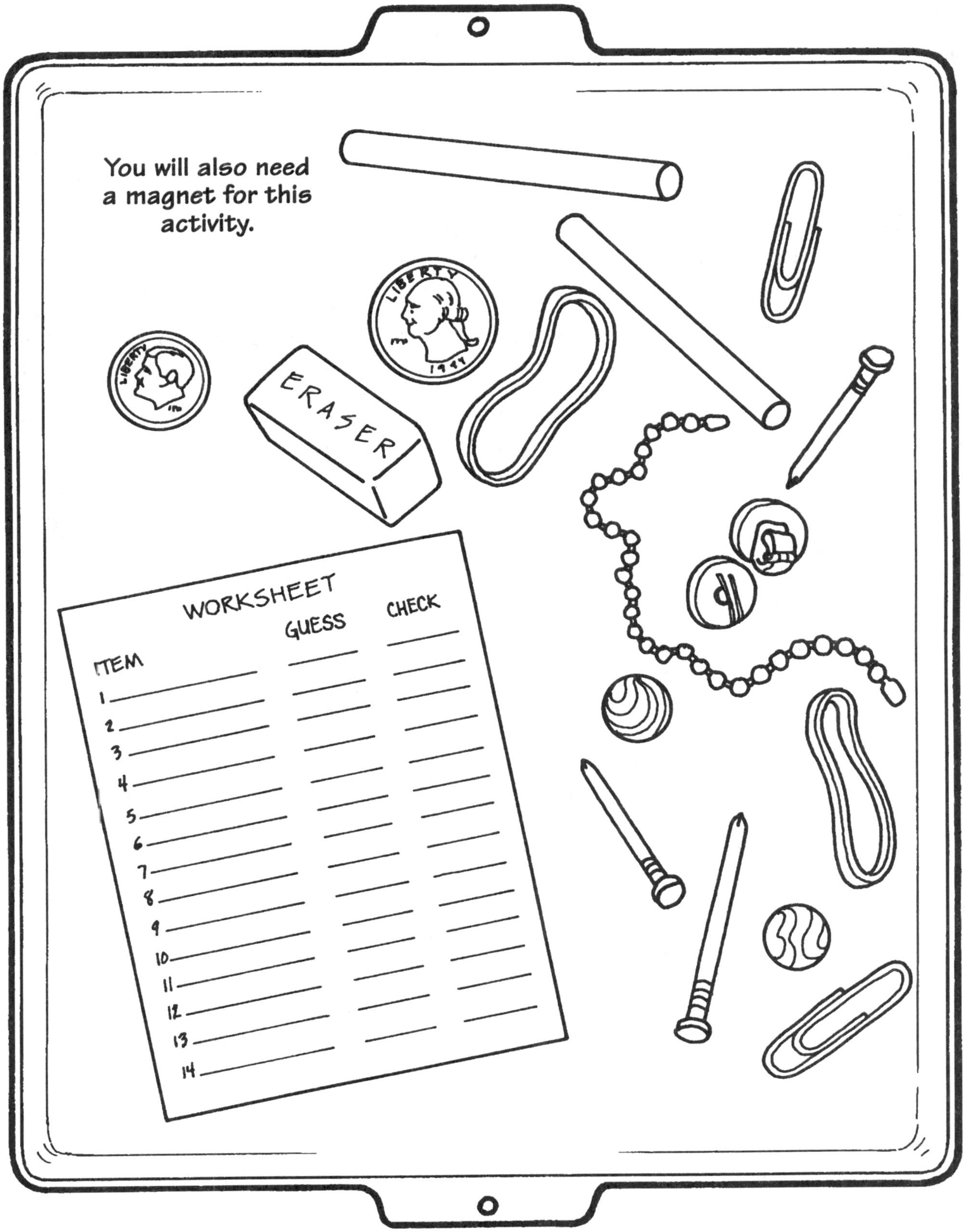

Machines and Simple Machines

Purpose: to introduce students to the idea of machines and simple machines and have them become acquainted with the various machines they see and use everyday

Skills: thinking, cooperating, observing, predicting, evaluating, and record keeping.

Materials: one copy of group worksheet (page 76) for each group, a variety of books on machines (optional for reading area, but a good idea for interest and motivation), one copy of "Home Machine Treasure Hunt" letter (page 77) for each student, copies of pages 78-81

Procedures: To begin this activity, hold a whole-class discussion about machines. List on the board all of the different kinds of machines that children know about or can think of. Explain very simply that a machine is something that helps us to work faster, or makes our work easier. Ask children to think about the kinds of machines they have in their homes and use the "Simple Machines" and "Machines at Home" masters to illustrate your whole-class discussion. Next, use either or both of these whole-classroom activities to illustrate the activity before moving into cooperative groups.

> **Simple Playground Machines:** It is easy to see examples of the most basic kind of machines, or simple machines, right on a school playground! Use the "Simple Machines" master on page 81 to let children see what simple machines look like. Then walk as a whole class out to your playground facility and discuss (and try) the simple machines there. (This is a good way to burn off a little excess energy before moving into cooperative groups too!)
>
> **Home Machine Demonstration:** Use the "Home Machines Illustrations" on pages 78 and 79 to show children a variety of machines, both with motors and without (people-powered). When describing machines that do not have motors, remember that while most non-motorized machines are people-powered, there are also a variety of machines that are animal-powered. (See illustration master on page 80.)
>
> Bring several people-powered machines and possibly machines with motors to use in a whole-class hands-on demonstration. Children love to investigate the way small machines like kitchen tools work and have a chance to try them themselves.
>
> After students have seen either or both of these demonstrations, have them work together in their own cooperative groups to complete their classroom "Machine Treasure Hunt." After a specified time, stop the groups and have each group's spokesperson read their list of machines. Give candy or stickers to the team that thinks of the most classroom machines.

 ©1995 Teacher Created Materials, Inc.

Machines and Simple Machines *(cont.)*

To Simplify: To simplify this activity, have students use the machine master illustrations as a guide and forego the class demonstration or playground exploration step.

To Expand: Have teams keep a running tally of their classroom machines list to see how many more they can think of over a week or a month or have students look for and list machines in other places like "machines in the city" or "machines on the farm."

Teacher Script: Today we are going to talk about machines. What is a machine? Can any of you tell me what you think? (*classroom discussion*) A machine is something that we use to make our work faster or easier. There are lots of machines that help us everywhere we look. There are two kinds of machines we are going to be thinking about for the next few days. We are going to think about machines with motors and machines without motors and people-or animal-powered machines. Let's look at the picture I have here. These are some machines with motors we probably have all seen before in our homes. Who can tell me what these are? Great. Let's think about as many others as we can.

> **Playground:** Now let's talk about simple machines. Simple machines are what you see here. What is this? Yes, it's a wheel. Did you know that a wheel is a kind of machine? Let's think of all the places we use wheels. (*Teacher models with other simple machines.*) Now I am going to show you a place where we have simple machines that I bet will surprise you. Let's all get our jackets and go outside. (*Teacher takes children to playground area and discusses and tries simple machines that are there.*)
>
> **Kitchen Machine Demonstration:** I have here a few machines from home. Can anyone tell me what this is? It's a broom. It is a people-powered machine. That means it doesn't have a motor. We make the power that makes it work with our bodies. Who wants to show us how this works? (*Teacher models a variety of household machines.*) Now let's all go into our cooperative groups and work together in looking around our classroom. We are going to try to think of as many machines in our classroom as we can and then write them down. Let's take 20 minutes to try this and, after we are finished, we will see which Science Club has the most. Let's go!

Evaluation and Processing: After teams have completed their lists, have them meet as a whole class and read their lists. Have prizes for all the teams or just the team with the largest machine list. Let children share what they liked best about the activity. To end this activity, give each child a "Home Machine Treasure Hunt" form to take home to hunt for machines with a parent or older brother or sister. Have children return these lists if you wish to see the results of their searches.

Machine Treasure Hunt!

Group Name ______________________________

With Motors	**Without Motors** (People-Powered)
______________	______________
______________	______________
______________	______________
______________	______________
______________	______________
______________	______________
______________	______________
______________	______________
______________	______________
______________	______________

Take a vote and write the name of your team's favorite machine here.

____

 ©1995 Teacher Created Materials, Inc.

Home Machine Treasure Hunt!

Dear Parents,

As part of our Cooperative Learning Science Unit, we are learning about machines. We have defined machines as both those with motors and those which are people-powered. As part of our unit, the children are asked to hunt for and name as many home machines as possible. This is an excellent way for them to reinforce what they have learned as well as relate it to their lives.

Use this activity sheet to work with your child on naming home machines.

________ Please return this activity sheet with your child to school.

________ Please enjoy this activity with your child and do not return this sheet.

Thank you,

____

- -

Machines

With Motors

______________________	______________________
______________________	______________________
______________________	______________________

No Motors—People-Powered

______________________	______________________
______________________	______________________
______________________	______________________

Person-Powered

Home Machines Illustrations

Broom

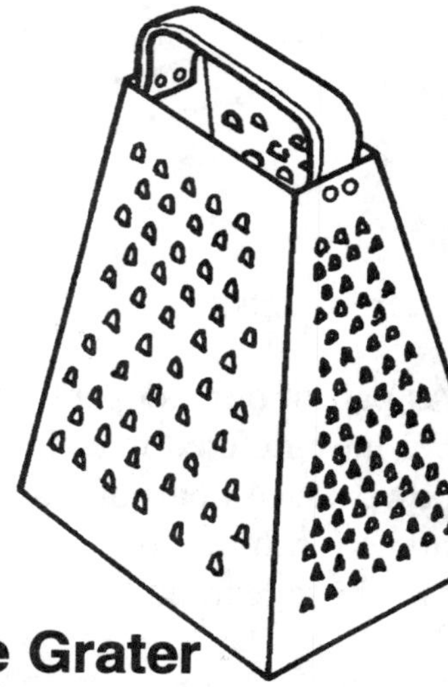

Cheese Grater

Potato Peeler

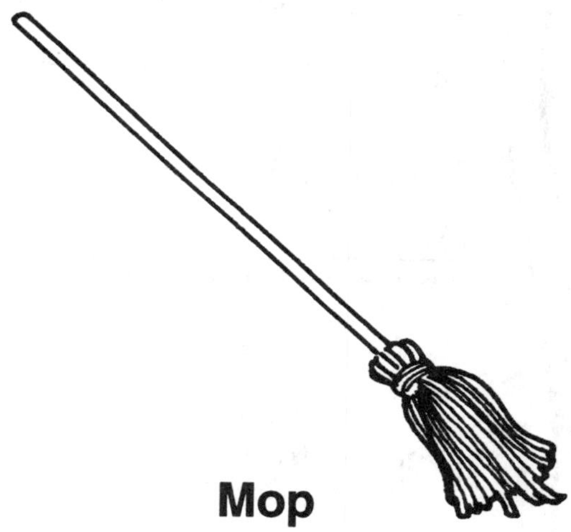

Mop

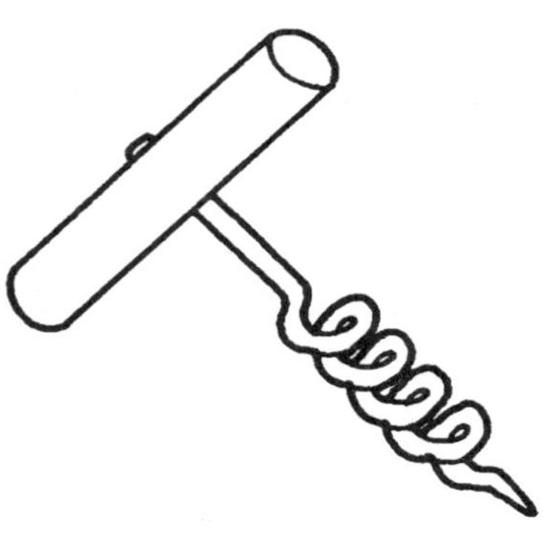

Corkscrew

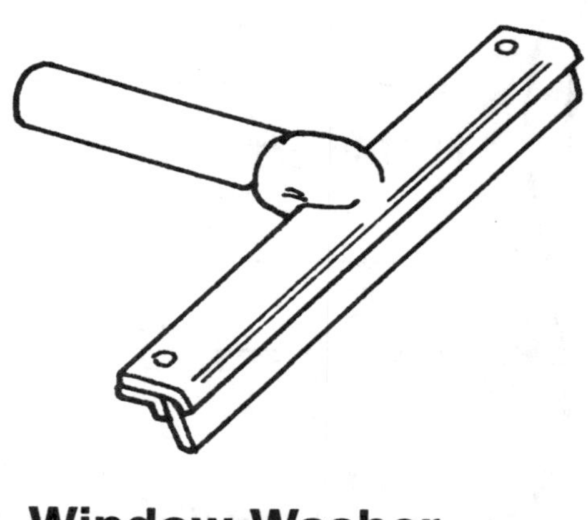

Window Washer

 ©1995 Teacher Created Materials, Inc.

Electric-Powered

Home Machines Illustrations

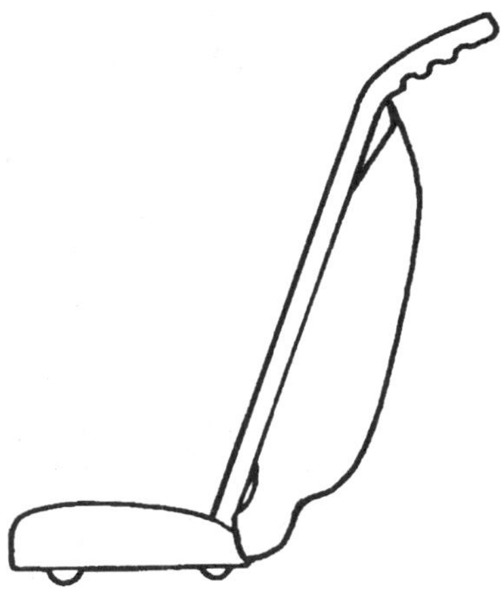

Vacuum

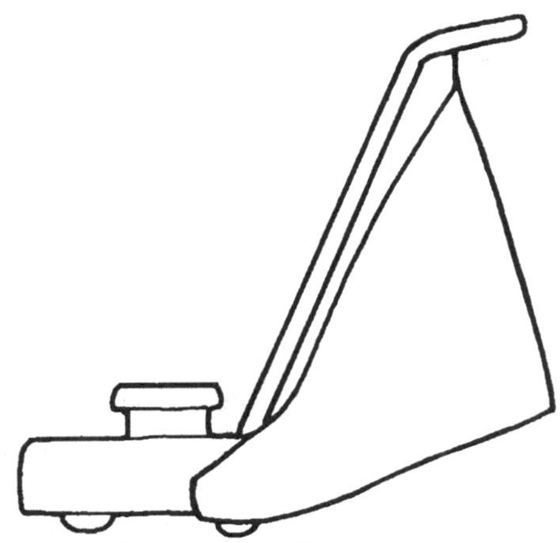

Lawn Mower

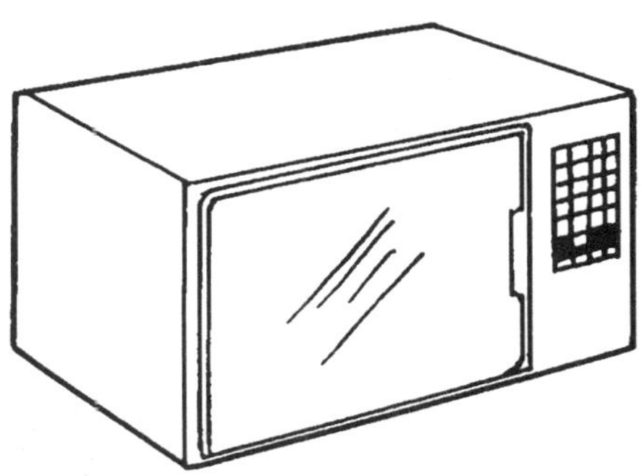

Microwave

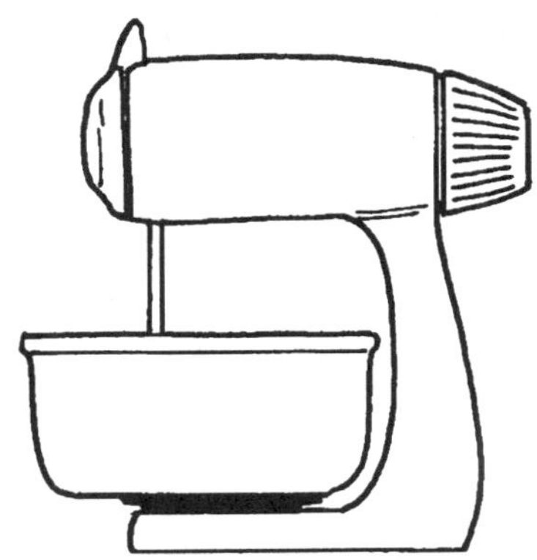

Electric Mixer

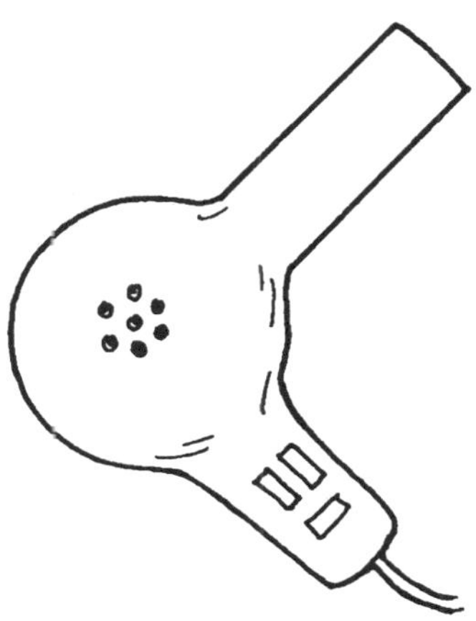

Blow Dryer

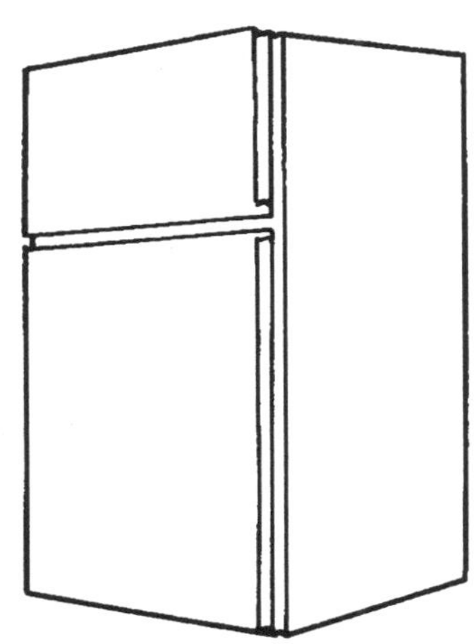

Refrigerator

Animal-Powered Machines

Plow

Wagon

 ©1995 Teacher Created Materials, Inc.

Simple Machines

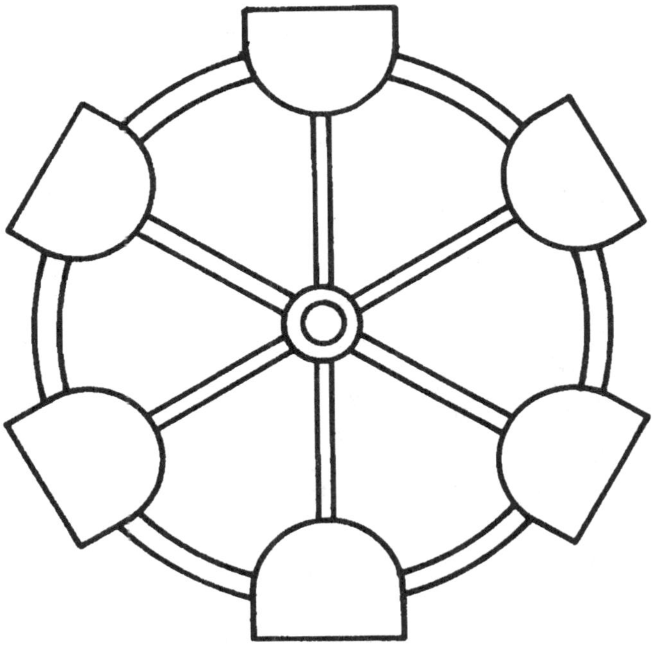

Ferris Wheel

Slide

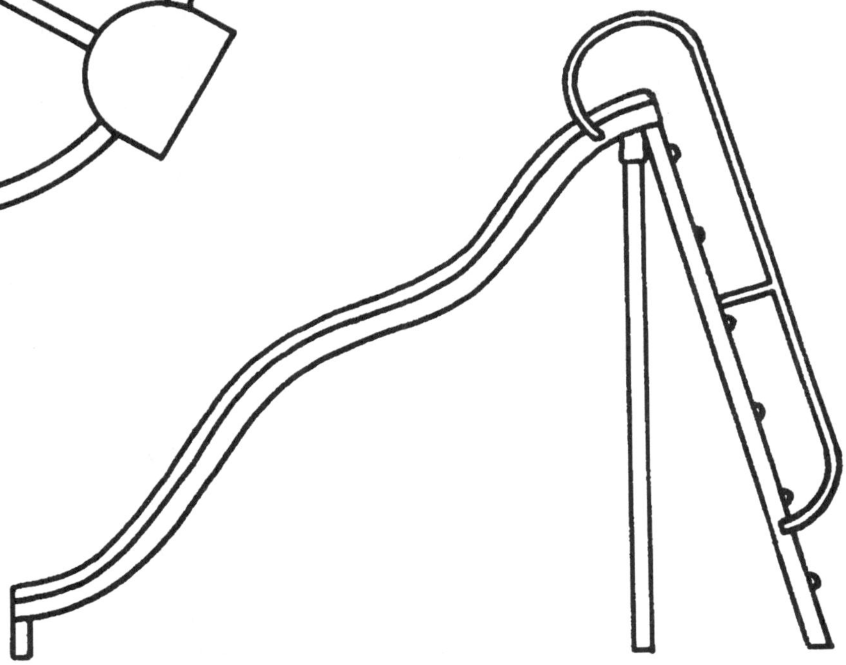

Teeter Totter

Machine Cookie Sheet

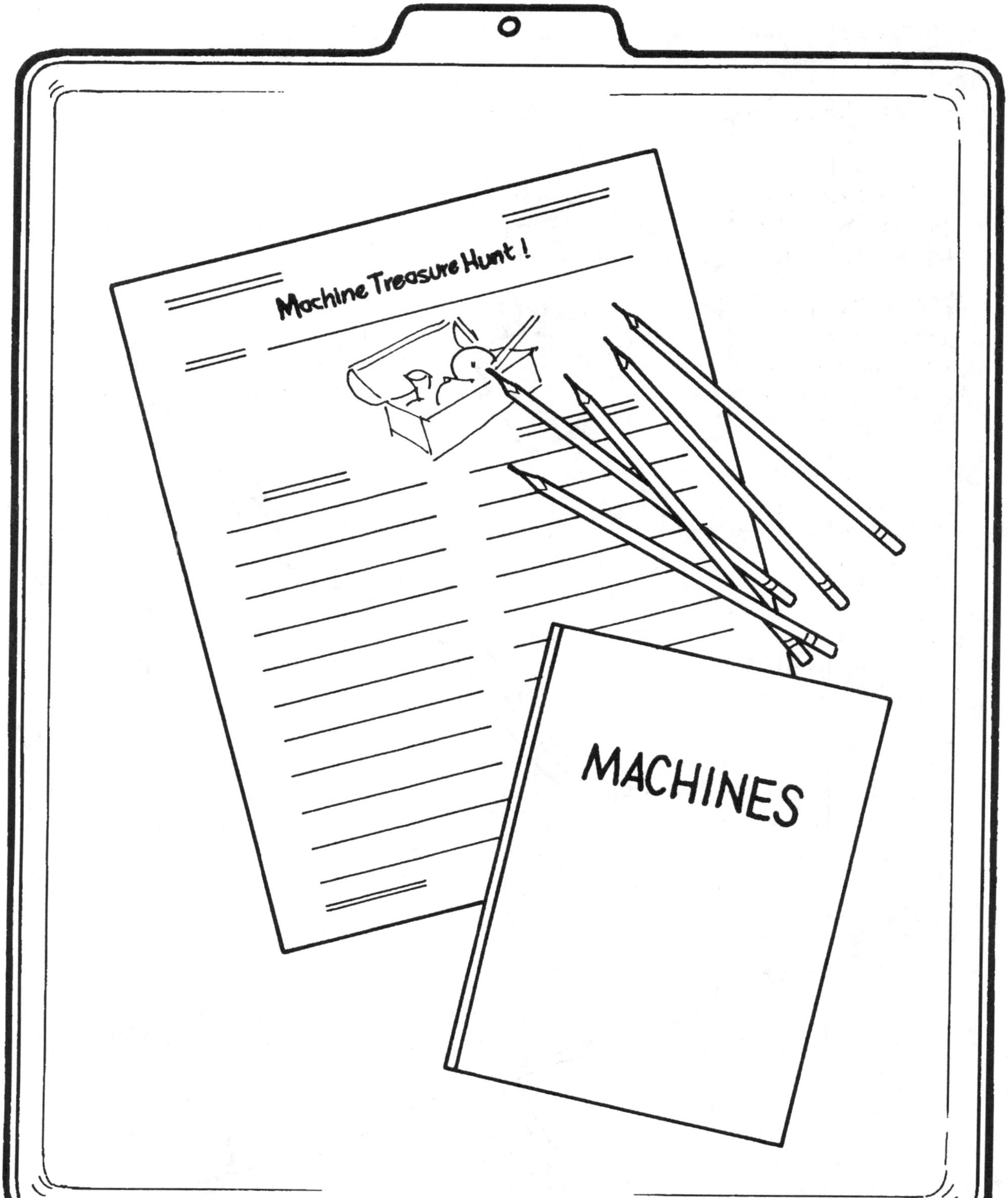

 ©1995 Teacher Created Materials, Inc.

Airplane Fun!

Purpose: to have hands-on experience using a simple machine and use the scientific method to record the investigation

Skills: thinking, cooperating, sharing, delegating, using logic, applying linear measurement skills, predicting, and graphing skills

Materials: for each group— a variety of paper to construct one airplane per student, copies of pages 86-88, a copy of page 90, ruler, tape measure or yardstick (to measure a large airplane flight space); for the teacher—one copy of page 89

Procedures: In this activity, each cooperative group will make and fly their own airplanes, reinforcing machine and scientific method concepts. This activity has a variety of steps. You will want to have an airplane unit that takes place over a week's time so you can break the cooperative tasks into smaller ones for the groups. (**Note:** *If using the metric system, convert measurement-related activities accordingly.*)

To begin this activity, hold a whole-class discussion reminding students about the machine activity and what they learned. Explain to students that airplanes got their name from the simple machine that makes up their wing, a plane. Hold a whole-class discussion about airplanes and flight. (You may wish to begin this activity by reading a story that excites children about airplanes such as *The Glorious Flight* by Alice and Martin Povensen.)

Explain to students that they will be making and flying their own airplanes. Students will fly them in their own groups and then determine which airplane is the fastest in the whole class. Divide the airplane unit into five days of smaller cooperative tasks as follows:

Day One

Before children create their own airplanes, model making a paper airplane in a whole-class discussion/demonstration. Have students move to their cooperative groups to construct their own airplanes. After students have made their airplanes in their groups, they will want to try test flights. Have materials on hand for children to make additional airplanes if their test flying loses or damages some of their airplanes.

Day Two

Have students work together to create and use their linear measurement skills to label their own airplane flying field. (You may wish to have one flying field and have all groups use it one group at a time or as teams.) For this portion of the activity, you will need ample space for students to work in. If you do not have outdoor access, consider an outdoor corridor or a side aisle in the multi-purpose room. You may wish students to work as a whole class to label only one airplane flight area. Students should work together to decide how big the space should be and how they should label the measurements. (To reinforce linear measurement skills, have children complete the activity on page 62, "Linear Measurement" before completing this activity.)

©1995 Teacher Created Materials, Inc.

Airplane Fun! *(cont.)*

Day Three

Have students work together in their cooperative groups using the "Prediction Page" to reinforce the skills they learned regarding prediction in the activity on page 62, "Guessing and Predicting." Students will make guesses regarding how far their own airplanes will fly and also which of the airplanes in their group will fly the farthest.

Day Four

Students work in their groups testing their airplanes to see how their guesses compare to what actually happens. Each group should decide which airplane is the best in their own group so they may enter it in the whole-class airplane flying competition. Students can also graph their results using the airplane graph on page 90.

Day Five

On the last day of the activity, have each group enter their best airplane into a whole-class flight contest. See which airplane flies the farthest and discuss why. Hand out Pilot Wings to each member of each group and follow up with an Airplane Party.

To Simplify:

Use one of the days as an isolated activity.

To Expand:

Have cooperative teams find out more about airplanes by going to the school or neighborhood library. Let cooperative groups work together and make presentations to the whole class about what they learned.

Teacher Script:

Day One

This week we are going to have a lot of fun learning about airplanes! We are going to make and fly our own airplanes and even have a contest to see whose airplane can fly the farthest. Today we are going to work together in our groups, and each of us is going to make a paper airplane. First, though, I am going to read a really interesting story about an airplane inventor. It is called *The Glorious Flight*. *(Teacher reads the story to the whole class.)* Now, I am going to show you several examples of planes that I have made, and we are all going to try to make an airplane together to get the hang of it. After we are finished, we will all go to our cooperative groups to make our airplanes. Then we will test them to see how they fly. *(Teacher models the process of making a paper airplane.)*

Now let's all move into our cooperative Science Club Groups and make our own airplanes. I will be available to help you all and see how you are doing. Let's go!

 ©1995 Teacher Created Materials, Inc.

Airplane Fun! *(cont.)*

Teacher Script: *(cont.)*

Day Two

Today we are going to use what we know about measurement to make our own airplane flying field. We are all going to use rulers, yardsticks, and measuring tapes to mark off a place to fly our planes. Let's remember about inches and feet and yards. (*Teacher holds whole-class discussion about linear measurement for review.*) Now, let me show you where we are going to make our flying field(s). *(Teacher should secure a large enough space, either inside or outdoors, that can be retained for the rest of the week.)* Now let's all work together to make our flying field!

Day Three

Today we are going to make predictions or guess what our airplanes will do. We are all going to talk about what we think will happen and make guesses and write them down. Tomorrow after we try our airplanes, we will be able to see how close our guesses came to what happens. Now let's all move into our groups and use this guessing activity sheet (Prediction Page) to write down our guesses. After we are finished, we will discuss them with the whole class.

Day Four

Today we are going to fly our airplanes in our groups and measure the distances they fly. We will then decide which plane is the fastest in each group. The fastest plane from each group will compete in our whole-class airplane flying contest. Now let's go try it. I will be available to groups that need help!

Day Five

Today we are going to find out which plane is the fastest. Each group has decided on a favorite plane. Let's put all the planes up here. Great! Now let's all go over to the airplane flying field and see what happens. After we are finished, we will have an airplane party! Let's go!

Evaluation and Processing: Follow up the end of this activity with a whole-class celebration and party. Give each student a copy of the certificate on page 91 to end the unit. Have a wonderful time! Remember to log the entire week on anecdotal record forms and put these and the airplanes (if you can get them) in children's portfolios.

How to Make a Paper Airplane

Follow the steps below to make a paper airplane. When your airplane is complete, use it with the activities on pages 87-90.

1. Place your paper sideways across your desk. Write letters A,B, and C on the paper like this:

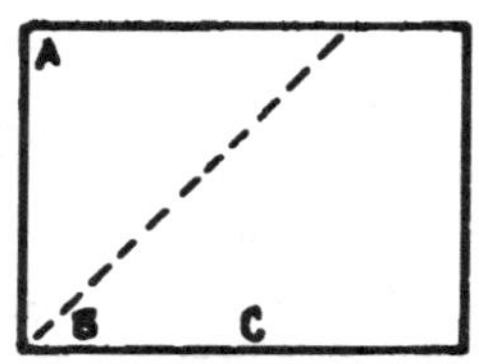

2. Fold corner A down to side C so that your paper looks like this:

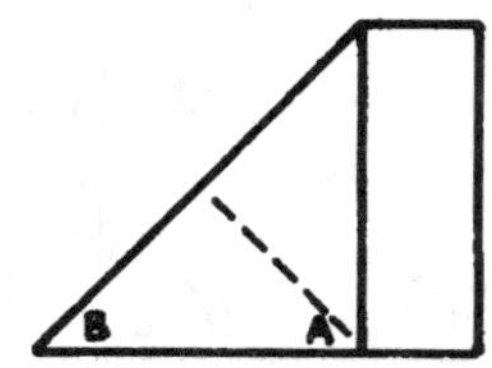

3. Fold up corner B to meet the top of the triangle section. (You have folded your triangle in half.) Your paper should look like this:

4. Fold the paper in half from top to bottom. Unfold. Your paper should look like this:

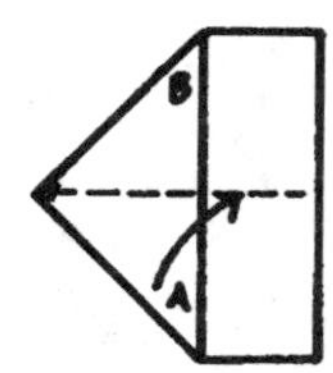

5. Fold the bottom edge of the triangle up so that it meets the center fold to make your airplane look like this:

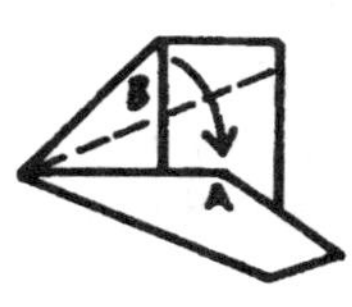

6. Fold the top edge of the triangle down so that it meets the center fold.

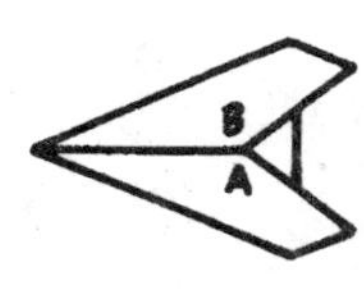

7. Turn the plane over. Your paper airplane should now look like this:

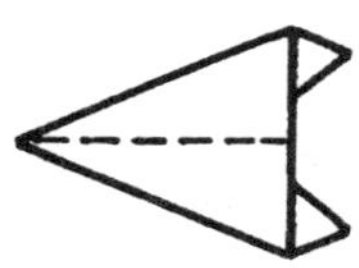

8. Fold up along the center fold.

Grasp the inside fold (center fold) with your hand, open the wings out, and fly your airplane!

 ©1995 Teacher Created Materials, Inc.

Airplane Fun Week!

Here is what your group should do:

Day One

1. Make a paper airplane, one for each member of your team.
2. Test fly your airplanes.

Day Two

3. Make your own airplane flying field; mark off feet and yards.

Day Three

4. Guess how far your airplanes will fly; use your "Prediction Page."

Day Four

5. Try your airplanes and write down what happens.
6. See whose airplane flies the farthest; graph the results.

Day Five

7. Use your fastest and best airplanes for a whole-class competition.
8. See which team's plane flies the farthest! Have a party!

Airplane Fun!

Group Name ____________________

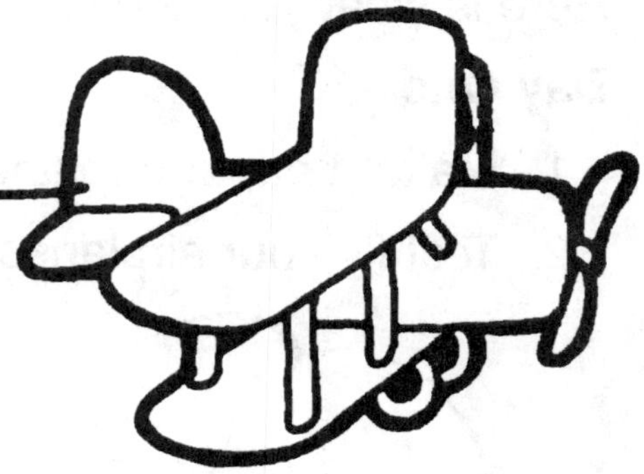

Prediction Page

Pilot Name ____

Plane Name ____

I think my plane will fly __________ feet __________ inches.

I think ______________________________'s plane will go the farthest.

Pilot Name ____

Plane Name ____

I think my plane will fly __________ feet __________ inches.

I think ______________________________'s plane will go the farthest.

Pilot Name ____

Plane Name ____

I think my plane will fly __________ feet __________ inches.

I think ______________________________'s plane will go the farthest.

Pilot Name ____

Plane Name ____

I think my plane will fly __________ feet __________ inches.

I think ______________________________'s plane will go the farthest.

Pilot Name ____

Plane Name ____

I think my plane will fly __________ feet __________ inches.

I think ______________________________'s plane will go the farthest.

 ©1995 Teacher Created Materials, Inc.

Airplane Flight Graph

Plane Name	0–1	1–2	2–3	3–4	4–5	5–6	6–7	7–8	8–9	9–10	10–11	11–12	12–13	13–14	14–15	15–16
Speed Machine																
Flying Ace																
Windmaster																
The Eagle																
Fast Flyer																

0 1 2 3 4 5 6 7 8 9 10 11 12 13 14 15 16

Feet

Group Name The Pilot Pals

Airplane Flight Graph

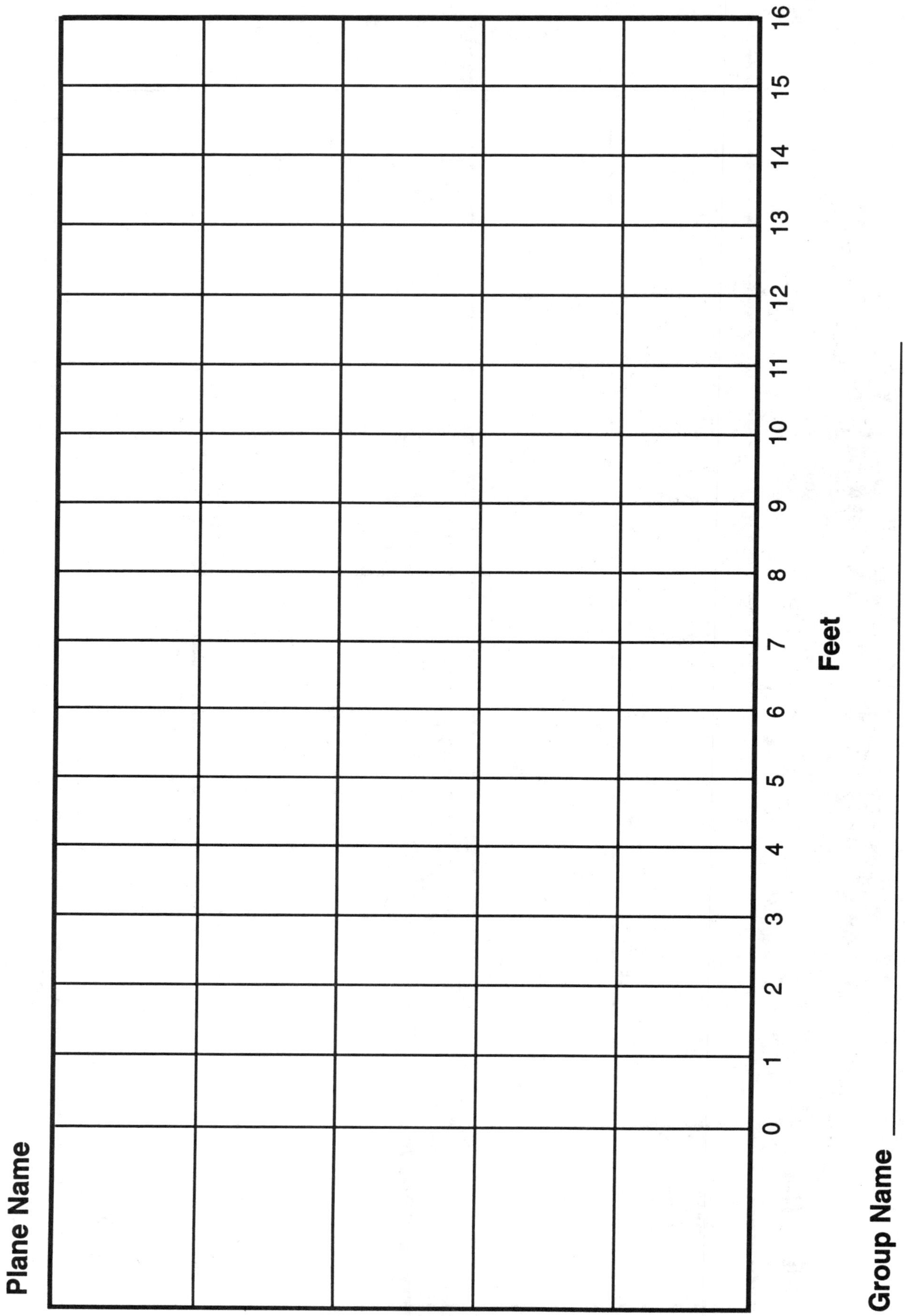

 ©1995 Teacher Created Materials, Inc.

WOW!

Name

is an Ace Pilot!

Date

Airplane Cookie Sheet

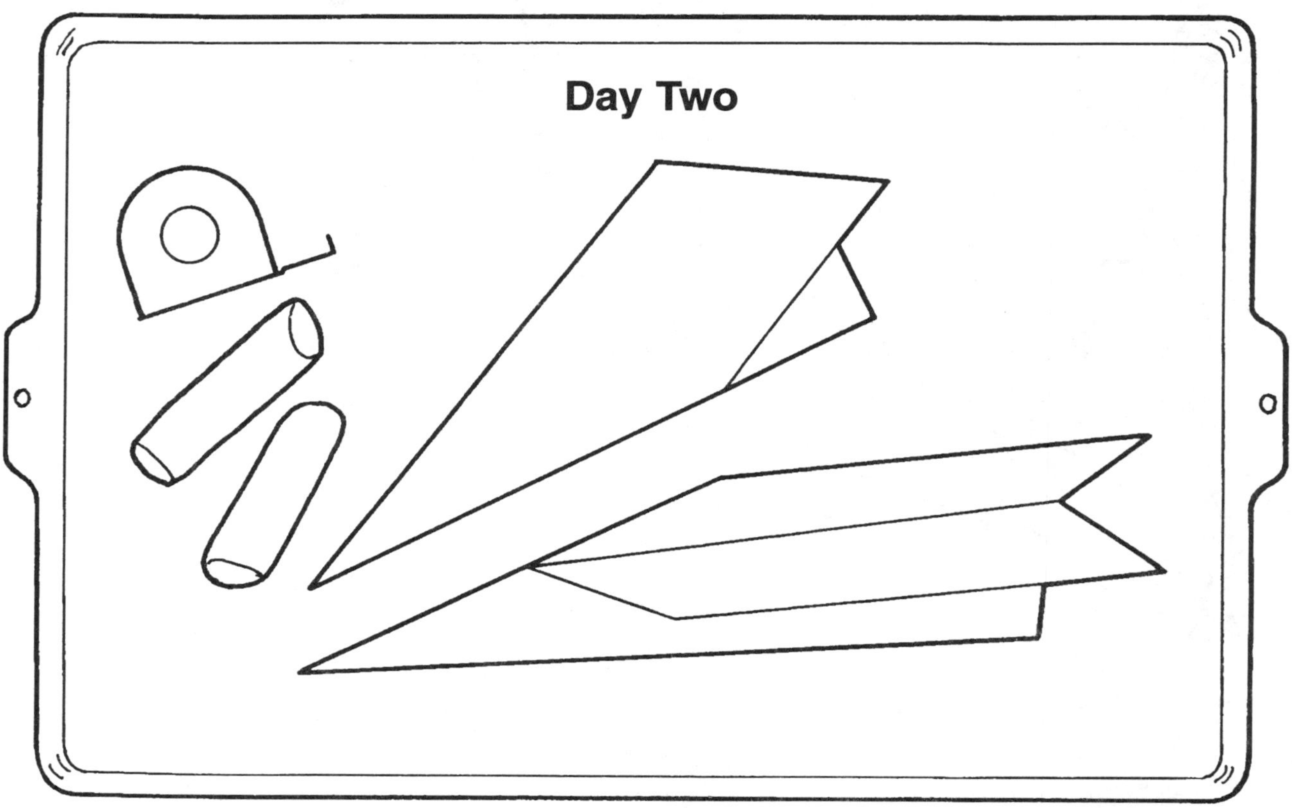

 ©1995 Teacher Created Materials, Inc.

Airplane Cookie Sheet (cont.)

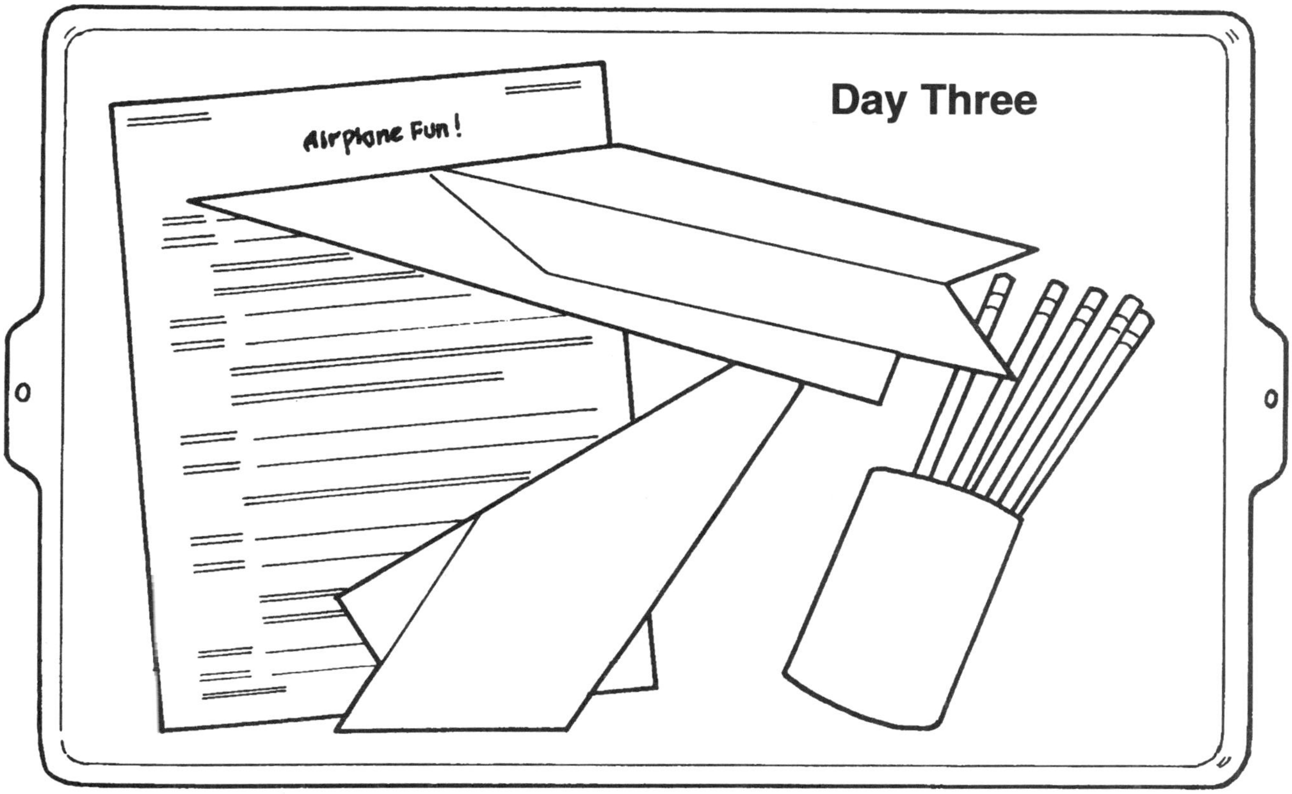

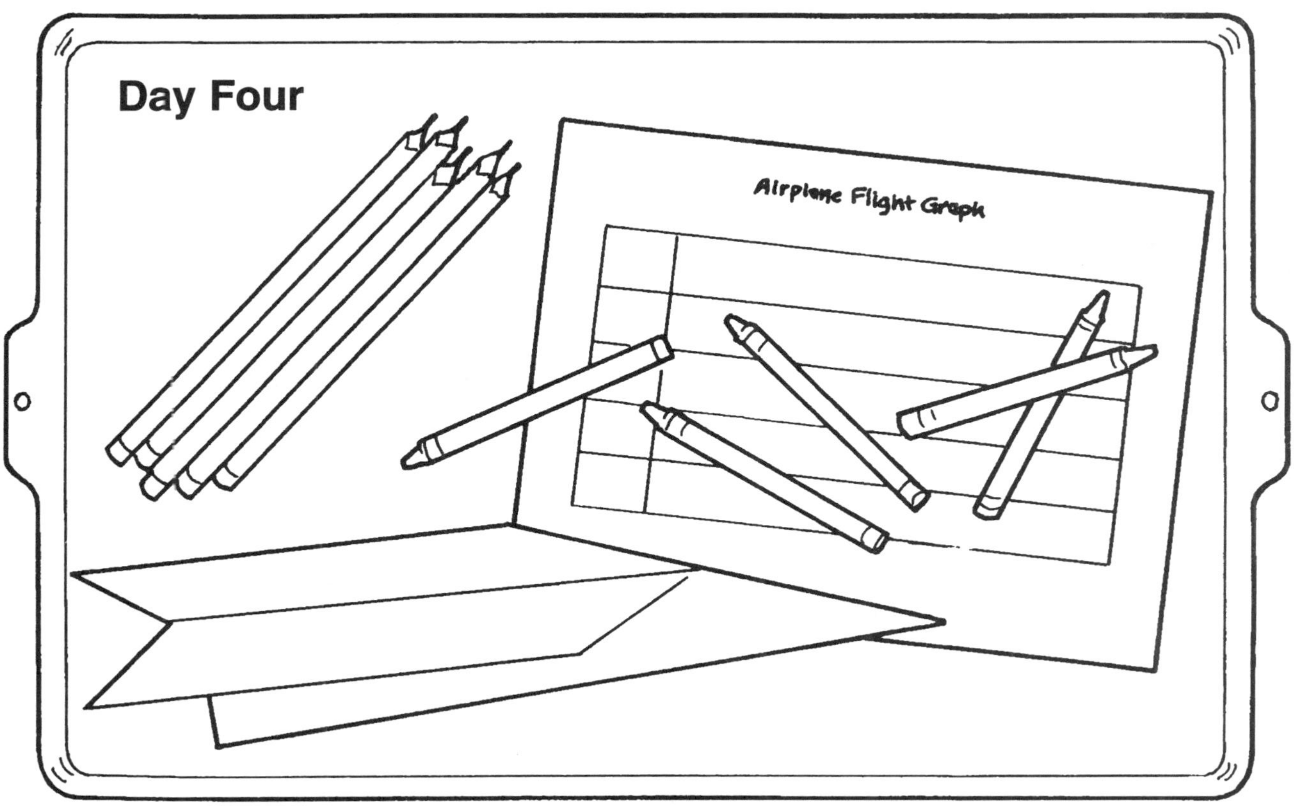

Sink or Float

Purpose: to understand the concept of buoyancy through a sinking and floating investigation and an art project

Skills: thinking, evaluating, cooperating, sharing, and observing

Materials: pencils, one glass jar with a lid for each student (toddler-sized baby food jars work very well for this activity and they make attractive, appropriately-sized paperweights), enough pebbles, beans, or shells to fill a quarter to a half of each container, waterproof glue, felt to cover the jar lids, a set of paperweight instructions (page 96) for each group, one copy of "Sink or Float" activity page (page 97) for each group, wrapping or tissue paper and ribbon

Procedures: In this activity, students explore the meanings of the words "sink" and "float," while creating a paperweight that can be used as an art project or a take-home gift. To begin this activity, hold a whole-class discussion regarding sinking and floating. Ask children to list things that sink and float in two separate columns on the chalkboard. After children understand the concept, model the paperweight-making activity. All that is needed are shells, pebbles, or beans to fill up half a small jar. Next, fill the jar with water and secure the lid. Turn the jar over to see whether the pebbles sink or float.

Have children work together to try the investigation, following the steps on their instruction sheet on page 96. As children get to the step where they are securing the lids of the jars with waterproof glue, you may wish to have a parent or adult helper assist with this part. (Some teachers will like to have an older student helper with each team for this activity.)

Have children meet again as a whole class and let teams discuss the activity and what happened in their own investigations.

To Simplify: Without making paperweights, have students try several items to see whether they sink or float as suggested in the first part of the "Sink or Float" activity page.

To Expand: Have students study boats by checking out books from your school or local library. Ask students to experiment on their own using a bowl of water and objects such as coins, washers, ping pong balls, etc. Have them make lists of objects that float and objects that sink.

 ©1995 Teacher Created Materials, Inc.

Sink or Float *(cont.)*

Teacher Script: Today we are going to experiment with things that sink or float. Let's talk about what sinks and what floats. *(Teacher holds a whole-class discussion, asking children to list things that sink or float.)* Now, here is something we are going to make today. While we are investigating what sinks and floats, we will also be making a special present we can take home to give to someone we love. This is a paperweight. After we do our sinking and floating investigation, we will talk about how to make them. Let's all move into our cooperative groups and try the investigation. I will walk around the room to help you.

Paperweight: Now that we have learned a lot about sinking and floating, we are going to make paperweights. A paperweight will be an attractive thing to take home and share with someone you love. You can tell them about our scientific investigation and what we learned. Let's all watch while I show you how I made this paperweight, and then you will make your own. The steps to make your paperweight are on a paper which looks like this on your cookie sheet. Let's see if you can all help each other follow these directions. *(Teacher models activity.)* Now let's try. When you are ready to glue the top on, I will help you put the waterproof glue on. Okay, here we go!

Evaluation and Processing: Have children meet as a whole class after their paperweights are finished and talk about the investigation. Have each group's spokesperson share about his/her team's investigation and what happened. Finish the activity by having children wrap their weights in colorful paper with a bow or ribbon.

Making a Paperweight

1. Get some shells, pebbles, or beans.

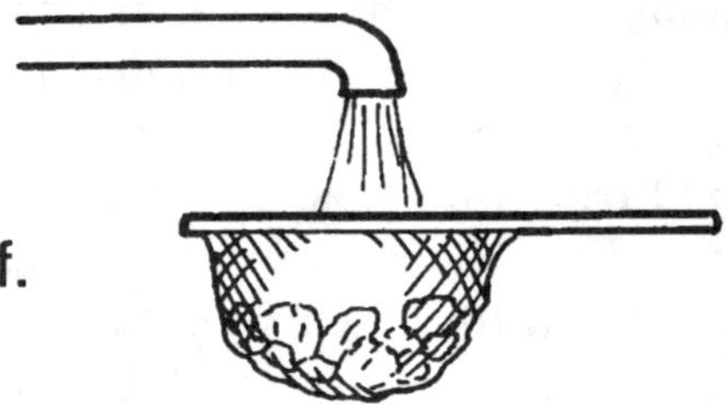

2. Wash them off.

3. Get a jar with a lid.

4. Put in the shells until the jar is half full.

5. Add water (and maybe food coloring).

6. Glue on the lid.

7. Glue felt on the lid so that it won't scratch your table.

8. Wrap it and give it to someone nice!

 ©1995 Teacher Created Materials, Inc.

Sink or Float

Group Name ____________________

1. Fill a glass with water.
2. Drop each of these things in the water and watch what happens.

1. What happened?

   ____

2. What happened?

   ____

3. What happened?

   ____

4. What happened?

   ____

5. What happened?

   ____

Sink or Float Cookie Sheet

 ©1995 Teacher Created Materials, Inc.

Make Your Own Zoo!

Purpose: to become familiar with animal life and habitats by taking a class field trip to the zoo and reproducing, in clay, a zoo model based on group research

Skills: research, observation, cooperation, sharing, consensus, and artistic skills

Materials: See individual days.

Procedures: In this activity, students research animals by taking notes and drawing pictures during a zoo field trip and then building a clay model of their own zoo. To introduce the activity, brainstorm an ABC list of zoo animals. Have student teams complete page 103, listing for each letter of the alphabet an animal whose name begins with that letter. Share group responses. Next, locate a nearby zoo and go through your school's procedures for taking a field trip. We have included a parent information and permission/volunteer letter on page 105 to make the process easier. Remember to pay close attention to zoo costs (for students and parent volunteers), eating facilities, wheelchair accommodations, and zoo hours. Explain about the zoo trip to your students. Send home the permission slip volunteer letter on page 105 a week or two before zoo week. This will give parents time to arrange their schedules to volunteer. (The help will be greatly appreciated.)

This activity will take a week with several pre-zoo-visit activities to get students enthused, and then the follow-up activities after the zoo visit will include making their own clay zoo. (See page 104 for a zoo week schedule.) The following is a five day activity description: (Remember to send the permission slip/

Day One: Zoo Safari Game

Before beginning this game with your cooperation groups, read *Dear Zoo* by Rod Campbell to get children excited about visiting the zoo and to get Zoo Week off to a great start!

Materials: pencils, a variety of research resources like encyclopedias and library books, one "Zoo Safari Game" (page 106) for each group, ten "Animal Facts" sheets (page 108) for each group (This sheet doubles for the pages in the students' "Zoo Picture Book.")

Directions: Have students use the "Zoo Safari Game" page to pick ten animals in which their group is interested. Provide books and other resources and drawing and coloring supplies for them to use as they find pictures of the animals and make their own team drawings. Have teams meet as a whole class to discuss the pictures each group has made and then bind the results in a book for a great Zoo Week display!

Make Your Own Zoo! *(cont.)*

Day Two: Zoo Picture Books

Materials: pencils, one "Zoo Picture Book" cover (page 107), ten "Animal Facts" pages for each student, brads, hole punch (or pre-punched holes), drawing materials

Directions: Have student groups prepare their own "Zoo Picture Books." Each student should color his/her book and put it away for the zoo field trip.

Day Three: Zoo Visit

Materials: "Zoo Picture Books," one for each child, pencils, and extra pencils for each adult leader

Directions: Before going to the zoo, review what you would like each team to do. Have each team work together at the zoo, making notes and drawing pictures of the animals they would like to make for their own clay zoo. Have students meet in teams before they leave for the zoo and brainstorm about the animals in which they think they will be interested. Remember to have each child wear his or her scientist badge so that you can keep everyone together.

Day Four: Clay Zoo Planning

Materials: pencils, completed "Zoo Picture Books," one "Clay Zoo Planner" (page 109) for each group

Directions: On this day, have each cooperative group work together to discuss what they saw at the zoo and make plans for their own clay zoo. Each group will use one copy of the "Clay Zoo Planner." Monitor and assist groups as needed.

Day Five: Making a Clay Zoo

Materials: one "Making a Clay Zoo" sheet (page 110) for each group, clay or salt dough, stiff cardboard or poster board, rocks and other environmental materials

Directions: Have groups work together to construct their own clay animals using the "Clay Zoo Planner" they completed the day before and the illustrated "Making a Clay Zoo" directions. You will want to have a variety of materials arranged on each team's cookie sheet. (See cookie sheet layout, page 112.) This part of the activity may take more than one group meeting session. After children have completed their zoos, make sure to give the clay ample drying time and then use the zoos as a wonderful Open House display.

 ©1995 Teacher Created Materials, Inc.

Make Your Own Zoo! (cont.)

To Simplify: Use any of this week's activities alone for a simple, cooperative, one-session experience.

To Expand: Use the zoo theme across your curriculum. Have children write zoo stories. Use illustrations from their "Zoo Picture Books" to make a colorful bulletin board display.

Teacher Script: This week we are going to have a lot of fun. This week is Zoo Week! We will be doing many wonderful things. We will be playing zoo games and learning about animals, drawing pictures of them, and even going on a trip to a real zoo! Then we will make our own clay zoos!

Zoo Week

❖ Day One: Zoo Safari Game

We are going to be playing a very exciting game in our cooperative groups today called the "Zoo Safari Game!" Before we start, I am going to read a wonderful story called *Dear Zoo* by Rod Campbell. This is a story about children who wanted to have pets from the zoo. Let's read this and see whether we can guess the animals. *(Teacher reads the book.)* Now, let's look at this activity page. There are a whole bunch of animals listed here. I want you all to go to your science groups and look at the list and decide on five *(or ten)* animals you would like to draw. Then I want you to work together and find out what the animals you picked look like. You might remember what they look like, but I want you to try to find a picture of the animal in one of our library books or our encyclopedias. If your team needs help finding pictures of the animals you want to draw, ask me or your older student helper to help you find one. After you draw a picture of the animal, work together to find some facts about that animal. You will need to figure together what is the most important thing to say about the animal. Let's go to our groups now and give it a try!

❖ Day Two: Zoo Picture Books

Today we are going to do something to help us get ready for our zoo trip. Scientists study things they want to find out about. That means they look very carefully and sometimes make pictures or write down facts. We are going to make picture books that we can take to the zoo. We will be able to make pictures of the animals we see and write down things about the animals so that we can remember what they did and where they lived. Has anyone here ever been to the zoo? Let's talk about what it was like so we can think about it before we go. *(Teacher holds a whole-class discussion about zoos and lets students share their ideas and memories of zoo visits. Teacher models how the "Zoo Animal Books" are put together.)*

Now let's all work in our groups to make our own picture books. After we have put together our zoo picture books, we will color the covers and put them away in a safe place for tomorrow. Let's begin!

Make Your Own Zoo! *(cont.)*

Zoo Week *(cont.)*

❖ *Day Three: Zoo Visit*

In just a little while, we are going to get on the bus that will take us to the zoo. Before we go, let's all sit in our groups and talk about what kind of animals we hope we will see. Be thinking about what kinds of animals you would like to make for your clay zoo while you talk about it.

At The Zoo: *(Teacher hands out "Zoo Picture Books" and pencils with erasers for each child.)* Now as you walk around the zoo in your Science Club Groups, make pictures of the animals you think you would like to make for your own clay zoo. Let's go!

After The Zoo: We really had a fun day. Let's all talk about what we saw in our groups, and then the groups will all come back together and talk about it. *(Have group and whole-class discussions.)*

❖ *Day Four: Clay Zoo Planning*

Now we are going to have fun planning our clay zoos. Let's all sit in our groups and use this planner to work together to figure out what our clay zoos will look like. Look at the pictures you made yesterday and talk about what you saw. You will all need to decide together what animals you will make for your zoo. If you need help, ask me. Let's start!

❖ *Day Five: Making a Clay Zoo*

Today we are going to make our zoos! Let's all sit in our groups and use the materials on the cookie sheets to work together to make the animals we chose in our group meetings yesterday. Look at the planner you completed and also at your picture books to help you make the animals. Let's all start. Ask your older student helper to help you or ask me. I can't wait to see our zoos! I know they're going to be wonderful!

Evaluation and Processing: You will want to give students the opportunity to give feedback and discuss each separate activity as well as to talk about how they felt about the whole week of activities. It is very important to use your anecdotal record form carefully during this week of activities and to make sure to date each entry. Also, there will be at least one individual storable item for each portfolio *(the "Zoo Picture Book")*.

 ©1995 Teacher Created Materials, Inc.

ABC Zoo Animals

A ____________________ N ____________________

B ____________________ O ____________________

C ____________________ P ____________________

D ____________________ Q ____________________

E ____________________ R ____________________

F ____________________ S ____________________

G ____________________ T ____________________

H ____________________ U ____________________

I ____________________ V ____________________

J ____________________ W ____________________

K ____________________ X ____________________

L ____________________ Y ____________________

M ____________________ Z ____________________

©1995 Teacher Created Materials, Inc.

Zoo Week Planner

One Week Before Zoo Week

Send out parent permission and volunteer letter.

Day One

"Zoo Safari Game"

Day Two

Prepare and color zoo picture books.

Day Three

Visit the zoo.

Day Four

Plan clay zoos.

Day Five

Make clay zoos.

 ©1995 Teacher Created Materials, Inc.

Dear Parents,

As part of our cooperative learning unit, we are studying zoos and zoo animals. Because of this, we are lucky enough to be taking a field trip to our local zoo. We are very excited about our zoo week, and we could use your help in a number of ways.

We need parent volunteers for the following tasks:

____

____

____

If you cannot work Zoo Week into your schedule, I am sure you will still hear a lot about it from your child! We plan to have a very exciting week. Please fill out the permission slip portion of this letter below and send it back to school with your child.

As usual, you are invited to volunteer, or to observe in any of our classes. Feel free to send your name and phone number on this form if you would like a call from me.

Sincerely,

____

- -

I authorize ________________________ to leave campus for a zoo field trip

on____________________.

Emergency contact:

______________________________________ Number: _______________

Please call me.

Name: __________________________________ Number: _______________

Best time to call: ______________________

Zoo Safari Game

1. Look at the words below.
2. With your group, pick ten of these animals.
3. Find out what they look like.
4. Draw pictures of them.
5. Find one fact about each animal.
   (Use dictionaries, library books, and encyclopedias to find out about the animals.)
6. If you have time, put the names of the animals in ABC order.

Snake
Lizard
Turtle
Crocodile
Seagull
Duck
Penguin
Eagle
Hawk
Sparrow
Flamingo
Parrot
Hummingbird
Ostrich
Owl
Whale
Dolphin
Seal
Otter
Fish
Shark
Eel
Sea Lion
Porpoise
Porcupine

Beaver
Skunk
Lion
Tiger
Wolf
Camel
Zebra
Horse
Kangaroo
Anteater
Llama
Bat

Woodpecker
Rabbit
Mouse
Bear
Squirrel
Toad
Frog
Cow
Goat
Sheep
Leopard
Monkey
Ape
Gorilla
Pig
Giraffe
Goose
Mongoose
Rhinoceros
Hippopotamus
Koala
Panda
Peacock
Iguana
Sloth

 ©1995 Teacher Created Materials, Inc.

Student Book

Zoo Picture Book

____

Group Name

____

Scientist's Name

Animal Facts

This is a picture of a/an__________________________________.

What is the most interesting thing about this animal?

____

____

In what kind of place does this animal live?

____

____

Some other interesting facts about this animal are:

1. ____
2. ____
3. ____

 ©1995 Teacher Created Materials, Inc.

Clay Zoo Planner

Group Name ______________________________

List the animals you saw at the zoo here:

1.____________	8.____________	15.____________
2.____________	9.____________	16.____________
3.____________	10.____________	17.____________
4.____________	11.____________	18.____________
5.____________	12.____________	19.____________
6.____________	13.____________	20.____________
7.____________	14.____________	21.____________

What five animals would your team like to make? (Each person should make one animal.)

Animal	Artist
1.	
2.	
3.	
4.	
5.	

What will your team use for the animal habitats (living places)?

Animal One ______________________________

Animal Two ______________________________

Animal Three ______________________________

Animal Four ______________________________

Animal Five ______________________________

Making a Clay Zoo

1. Decide with your group what animals you will make.

2. Plan what their habitats (living places) will look like.

   You can use these things to make animal habitats.

   - paper
   - paint
   - clay
   - sand
   - crayons
   - cotton
   - pipe cleaners
   - nature samples

3. Make your clay animals.

   Look at books and your pictures from the zoo to remember how the animals look.

4. Let the animals dry.

5. Paint or decorate your animals.

6. Put your animals in their zoo.

7. Show your class!

 ©1995 Teacher Created Materials, Inc.

Zoo Cookie Sheet

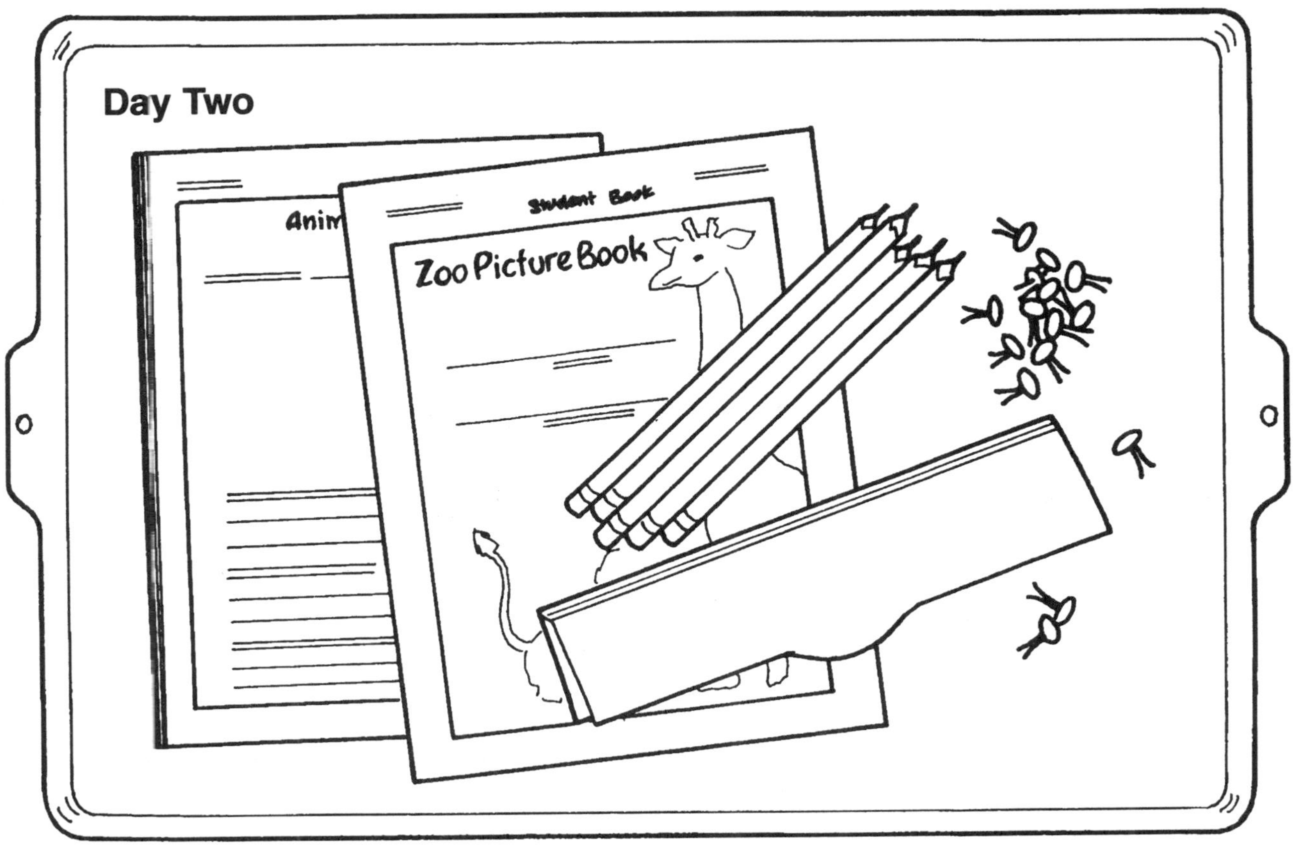

Zoo Cookie Sheet *(cont.)*

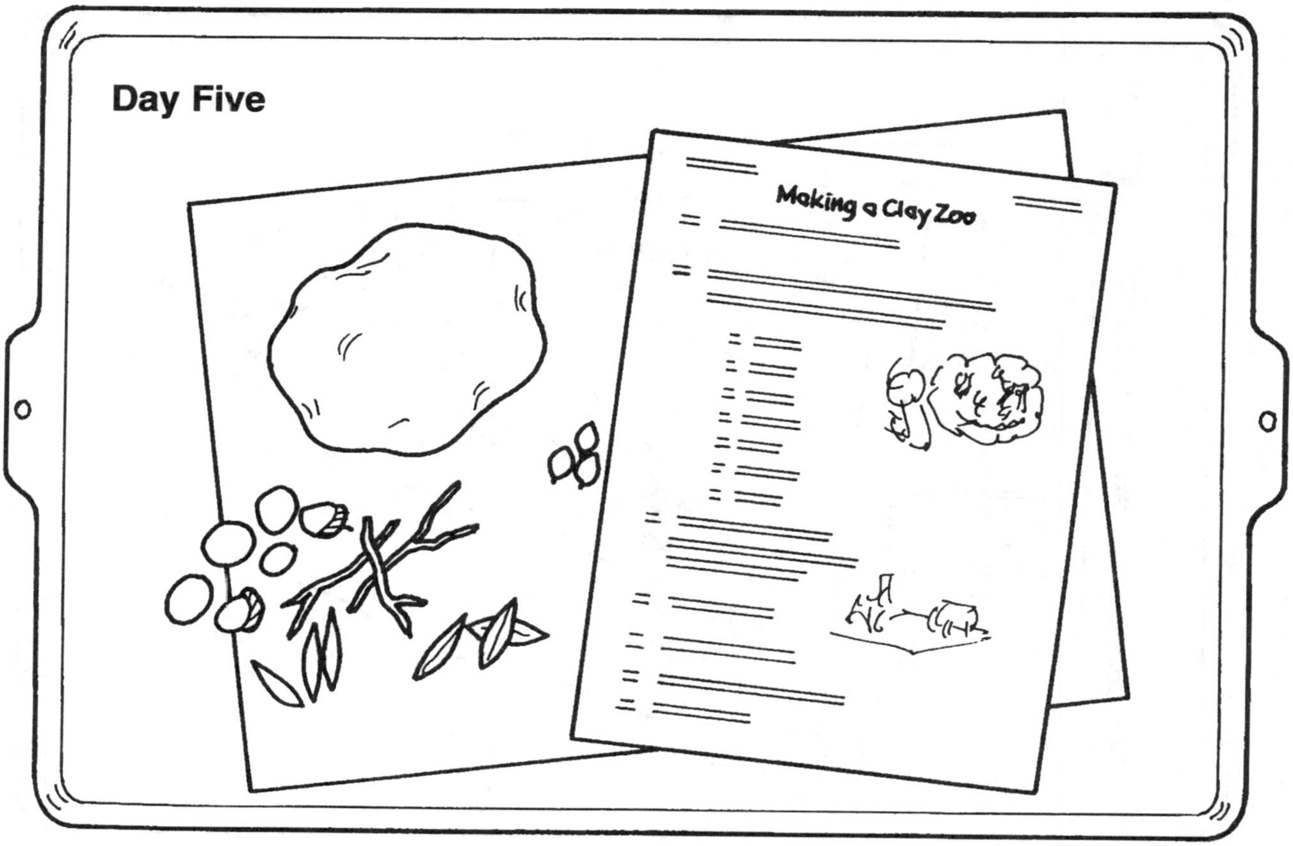

Wind! Making Pinwheels

Purpose: to become aware of weather conditions like wind by creating and using a pinwheel

Skills: planning, thinking logically, sequencing, demonstrating teamwork, observing, evaluating, exhibiting oral and written communication skills

Materials: one copy of "Student Pinwheel Picture Directions" (page 116) for each group, one copy of "Pinwheel Master" (page 117) for each child, one pencil and a straight pin for each child, one copy of the wind illustration on page 118 (enlarged for whole-class discussion), one copy of "Pinwheel Exploration" sheet (page 119) for each group

Procedures: In this activity, students study wind by making and using their own pinwheels. Begin the activity by having a whole-class discussion about wind. Discuss with students what they like about it. Talk about what happens when the wind blows. Make a classroom list of everything that the wind can blow. Explain to children that the air is always moving around us and that it moves because the air temperature is different in different places.

Have the whole class walk outside or to an open window and do a simple scientific demonstration.

1. Lick the tip of your finger.
2. Hold it in the air.
3. Which way is the wind blowing?

Come to consensus about which way the wind is blowing. Let students share their opinions.

Next, model the steps in making a pinwheel. This activity will require some adult or older student assistance in the final stages. It should not be done with children who will not treat the pins carefully. You will know what the level of awareness and responsibility is in your own classroom.

Follow the Teacher Instructions for Making Pinwheels on page 115. While you are modeling this activity, ask children to look at their own picture instructions on page 116 and find each step as you demonstrate it.

After the children have seen how to make a pinwheel, have cooperative groups work together to make their own pinwheels. Next, brainstorm a list of the places outside where they would like to try their pinwheels. Have each group narrow their own list down to five places for their actual exploration on page 119.

Wind! Making Pinwheels *(cont.)*

To Simplify: To simplify this activity, make the pinwheels and distribute these to teams so that they are already prepared for the investigation step.

To Expand: Have children color their pinwheels with a variety of designs to make them more interesting as they spin. You may also wish to fly a kite, hang a class windsock, study windmills, hang a wind chime, gather magazine pictures of the wind, learn about hurricanes, tornados, and cyclones, or read the daily weather report.

Teacher Script: Today we are going to learn about wind and then we are going to do a really fascinating investigation with pinwheels! We are each going to make one of these and use it to study the wind.

Let's talk about the wind first. What do you like about the wind? *(discussion)* Let's name as many things as we can that the wind blows and list them here. *(discussion)* Let's add to this list all day as we think about it.

I have a picture here that shows us why the wind blows. Let's all look at it together. The air is always moving. It moves because the air temperature is different in different places. This picture shows the cool air moving down and the warm air moving up. This is how wind happens.

Now, I am going to show you the steps in making a pinwheel. Look at your own direction sheet and follow the picture steps as I do them. Then we will move into our groups and make our own pinwheels. *(Teacher models the process and has children discuss the steps as a whole class.)* Now let's all make our pinwheels. I will help you with the hard parts.

Brainstorming

(This can be done on a separate day, if you wish.)

Now let's use our brains to think of as many places as we can where we would like to put our pinwheels to see how they work. This is called brainstorming. When we brainstorm we think of as many ideas as we can. There are no right ideas or wrong ideas in brainstorming. Every idea is good.

After Brainstorming

While you were brainstorming, you thought of many places to put your pinwheels. Look carefully at your ideas and pick five. You need to all decide together. Write the five places on this "Pinwheel Exploration" page. If you can't decide, I will help you.

 ©1995 Teacher Created Materials, Inc.

Wind! Making Pinwheels *(cont.)*

Teacher Script: *(cont.)*

After Brainstorming *(cont.)*

It is time to try our new pinwheels! We will all go outside with our older student helpers and try using our pinwheels in the areas we decided on in our groups. Hold them or stick them in the ground and watch what happens. Remember to write what happens on your group's worksheet.

Evaluation and Processing: Have children meet as a whole class to discuss what happened when they tried their pinwheels. Let them compare the similarities and differences between their own group's and other group's investigations. (Remember to use the "Indiviual Anecdotal Record" on page 17 to keep accurate records.) Children will enjoy keeping their pinwheels and playing with them, so if you would like to have a work example for their portfolios, have each child make two.

Teacher Instructions for Making Pinwheels

1. Print enough copies of page 117 so that each child has at least one pinwheel. (There are two pinwheels on each page.) Each child will need a new, unsharpened pencil with an eraser and a straight pin.
2. Have students carefully cut along the lines. Remind them not to cut inside the circle!
3. Bend each of the "x" marked edges into the center of the circle.
4. Place the pinwheel flat on a table and put a finger on each of the edges and hold.
5. Carefully push a straight pin into the center.
6. Push the end of the pin into the eraser with the pencil lying flat on the table. Do not push the pin point all the way through the eraser.
7. Blow!

Student Pinwheel Picture Directions

1.

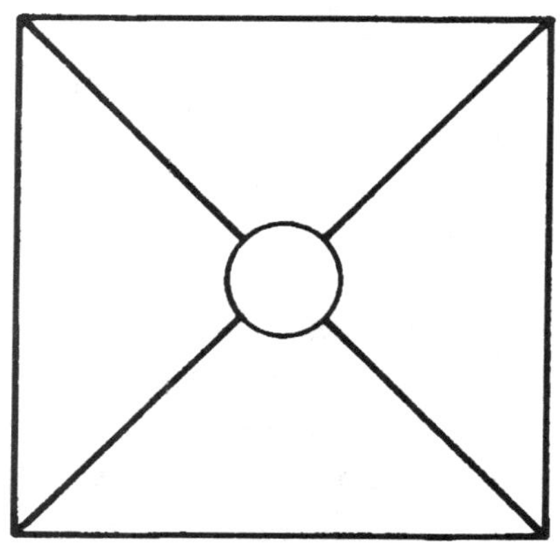

2.

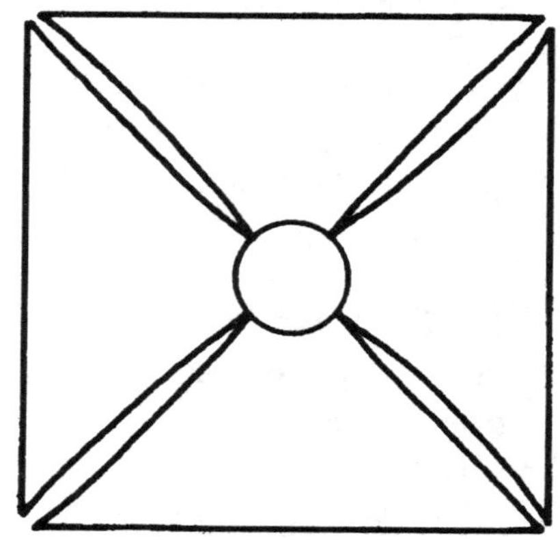

3.

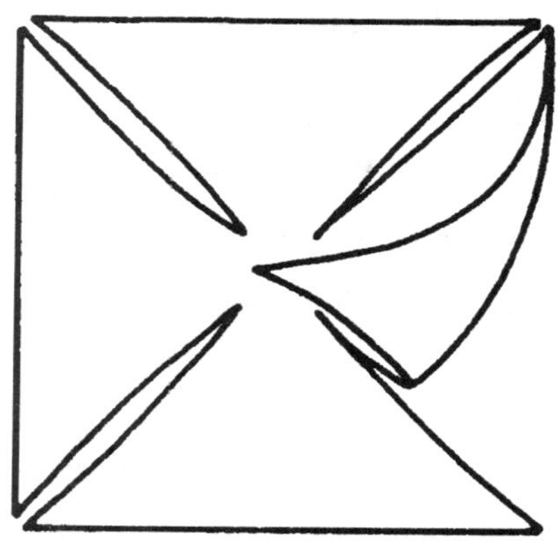

4.

5.

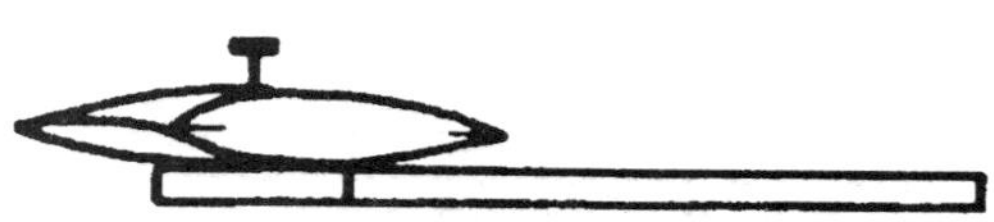

6.

 ©1995 Teacher Created Materials, Inc.

Pinwheel Master

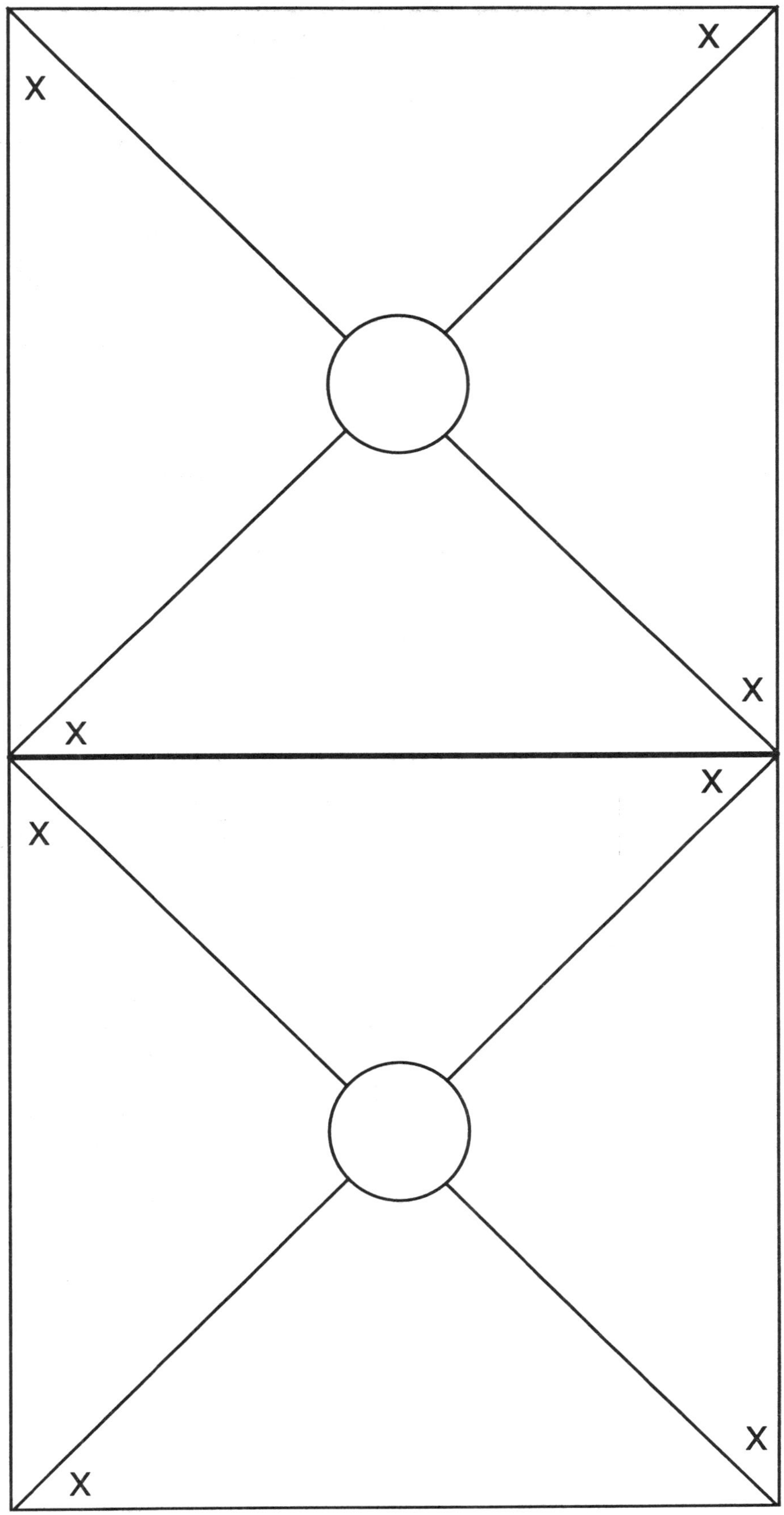

Wind Illustration

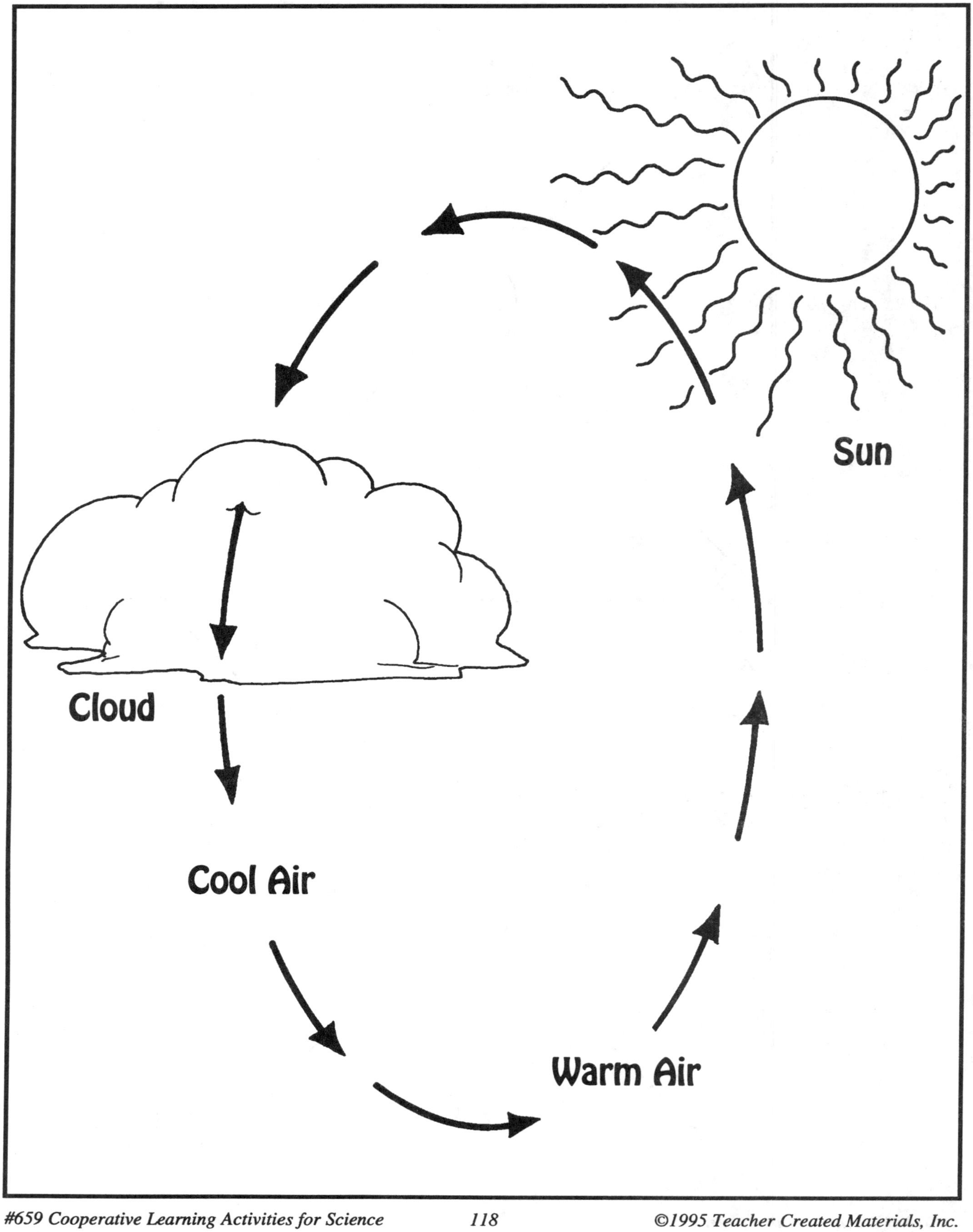

 ©1995 Teacher Created Materials, Inc.

Pinwheel Exploration

Group Name ______________________________

What happens when you blow on your pinwheel?

____

____

Where do you think is the best place to put your pinwheel so that the wind catches it?

1. ______________________________
2. ______________________________
3. ______________________________
4. ______________________________
5. ______________________________

Try each of these places and tell what happens.

1. ______________________________
2. ______________________________
3. ______________________________
4. ______________________________
5. ______________________________

©1995 Teacher Created Materials, Inc.

Pinwheel Cookie Sheet

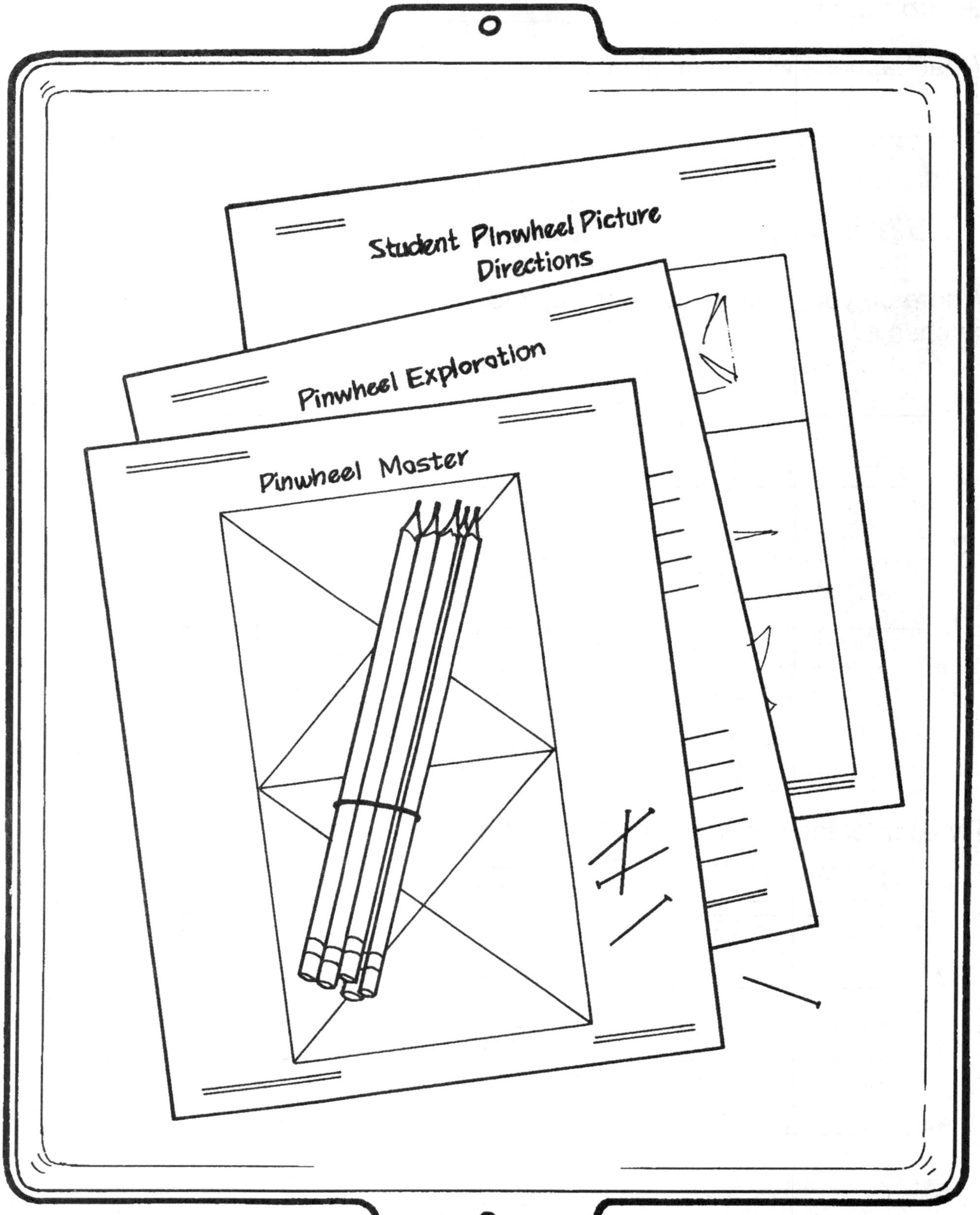

 ©1995 Teacher Created Materials, Inc.

Seasons

Shoebox Season Scenes

Purpose: to become aware of seasonal changes by learning about the four seasons and culminating in the making of shoebox weather scenes

Skills: observing, cooperating, demonstrating oral and written language skills, and artistic skills

Materials: season activity pages 125–128 (one set of four for each group), season pictures (one for each group as chosen by children), one copy of "Shoebox Weather Figures" (page 133) for each group, one shoebox for each group, one copy of "Shoebox Planner" (page134) for each group, one copy of "Shoebox Directions" (page 135) for each group, glue, scissors, art supplies, books listed by day for each of the four seasons

Procedures: In this activity, children will spend a week learning about the four seasons and culminate the activity by making a group shoebox season scene. Begin this activity by holding a whole-class discussion about the seasons and reading *When Summer Ends* by Susi and Gregg Fowler. This book acquaints children with the seasons and is an excellent way to start this week.

Explain to the children that they will be spending a day learning about each season. At the end of the week they will decide in their groups which is their favorite season. Then they will make a shoebox season scene illustrating the season they chose.

(This activity is written to span a week; however, it is possible to use the activities separately or seasonally, if you wish.)

The following is a list of activities for each day:

Day One

Hold a whole-class discussion about the seasons. Read *When Summer Ends*. Have children work together in cooperative groups to discuss what they know about fall and to fill out their "Fall" activity page.

Day Two

Hold a whole-class discussion about winter. Read *Something is Going to Happen* by Charlotte Zololow. Have children discuss what they know about winter and fill out the "Winter" activity page.

Seasons (cont.)

Day Three

Hold a whole-class discussion about spring. Then read *My Spring Robin* by Anne Rockwell to the students and have them work together on the "Spring" activity page in their cooperative groups.

Day Four

Have a whole-class discussion about summer and read *The Seasons of Arnold's Apple Tree* by Gail Gibbons. Have children work together in their cooperative groups on the "Summer" activity page.

Day Five

Model the "Shoebox Directions" sheet on page 135. Have children work together in their cooperative groups, first to decide what season they would like to depict and then to plan what their shoeboxes will look like. Have them use the "Shoebox Planner" to simplify their group decision-making and planning process.

After their shoeboxes are finished, let groups share, discuss, and display them.

To Simplify: Use one of the activities for the current season and have student groups depict just that season in their shoebox scenes.

To Expand: Plan seasonal clothing days. Have children bring picture examples of clothing appropriate for each season or have teams draw murals for each season. Have a "Winter in July," or a "Day at the Beach" theme for a day in winter.

Teacher Script:

Day One

This week we are going to learn about the seasons. Let's listen to a story titled *When Summer Ends*. It is about the seasons. Then we will talk about them. *(Teacher reads story.)* Now let's talk a little bit about the seasons. What happens when the seasons change? Can anyone tell me what season it is right now? Great. Today we are going to talk about fall in our Science Club groups. You will all talk about what you know about fall. *(Teacher may wish to discuss the particular season at length in class discussion for clarity.)* Let's go to your groups and talk about fall and use your activity page to help you.

 ©1995 Teacher Created Materials, Inc.

Seasons *(cont.)*

Teacher Script: *(cont.)*

Day Two

Today we are going to study the season called winter. I'm sure we know a lot about what happens in winter. Winter is an exciting season. I am going to read a story called *Something is Going to Happen*. After I read it, we will talk about winter in our cooperative groups. *(Teacher reads the story and models the discussion.)*

Day Three

Today we are going to learn about spring. I have another wonderful story called *My Spring Robin*. Let's listen to the story and then talk about spring in our cooperative groups.

Day Four

Today we are going to talk about summer. Let's start by reading a book called *The Seasons of Arnold's Apple Tree*. This book will remind us about all of the seasons as they continue to happen, one right after the other. Then we will fill out our "Summer" activity pages in our cooperative groups. I want you all to be thinking and talking about what season you would like to choose for your shoebox scene. You will be able to do only one season, so you will need to work in your groups to pick one you can all agree on.

Day Five

Today we are going to make our shoebox scenes. First, let's all work together in our groups and plan what we will do. Use your planning page to plan your shoebox scene. Then we will all make a shoebox scene. *(Teacher models a prepared shoebox and explains how they are made and what materials to use.)* Okay, let's start!

(You may wish to continue the actual making of the shoebox scene over several days, if necessary. Also, these make excellent displays for your Science Club Center during Open House.)

Evaluation and Processing:

You may wish to process with your whole class daily, as this is a long activity, rather than to wait until it ends. Remember to use your anecdotal record form throughout this activity so that it will be easier to remember what happens.

©1995 Teacher Created Materials, Inc.

The Seasons Week Schedule

Day One

Overview

Fall Story and Activity Page

Day Two

Winter Story and Activity Page

Day Three

Spring Story and Activity Page

Day Four

Summer Story and Activity Page

Day Five

Plan and Make Shoebox Scenes

 ©1995 Teacher Created Materials, Inc.

Fall

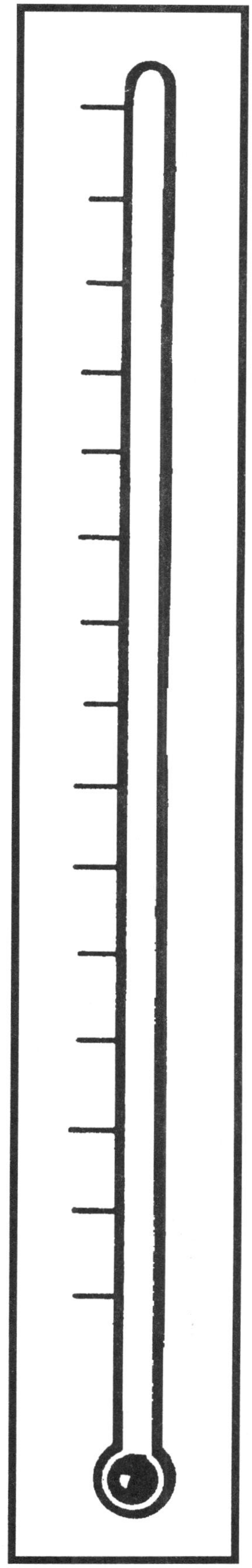

Group Name____

What does fall look like? Describe five ways fall looks to you.

1. ____
2. ____
3. ____
4. ____
5. ____

What kinds of clothes do we wear in the fall?

____

____

____

What kinds of weather do we have in the fall?

____

____

____

What is the temperature in the fall? Show it on the thermometer on this page. ____________________________

©1995 Teacher Created Materials, Inc.

Winter

Group Name______________________________

What does winter look like? Describe five ways winter looks to you.

1. ______________________________
2. ______________________________
3. ______________________________
4. ______________________________
5. ______________________________

What kinds of clothes do we wear in the winter?

____

____

____

What kinds of weather do we have in the winter?

____

____

____

What is the temperature in the winter? Show it on the thermometer on this page. ______________________________

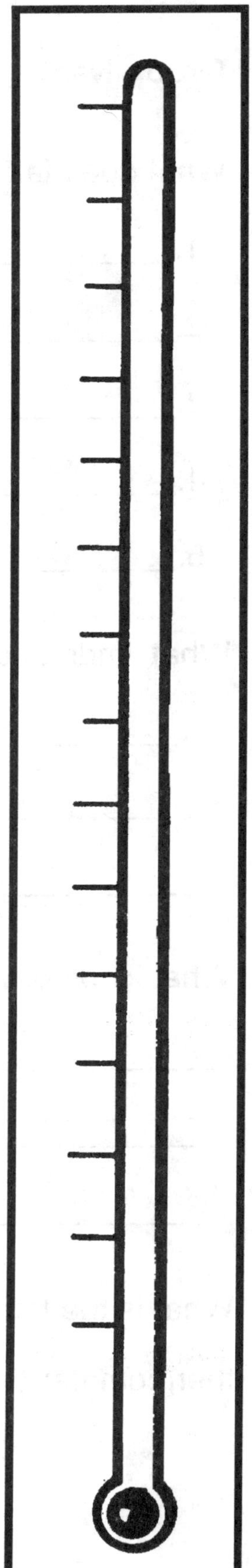

©1995 Teacher Created Materials, Inc.

Spring

Group Name____

What does spring look like? Describe five ways spring looks to you.

1.____

2.____

3.____

4.____

5.____

What kinds of clothes do we wear in the spring?

What kinds of weather do we have in the spring?

What is the temperature in the spring? Show it on the thermometer on this page. ________________________

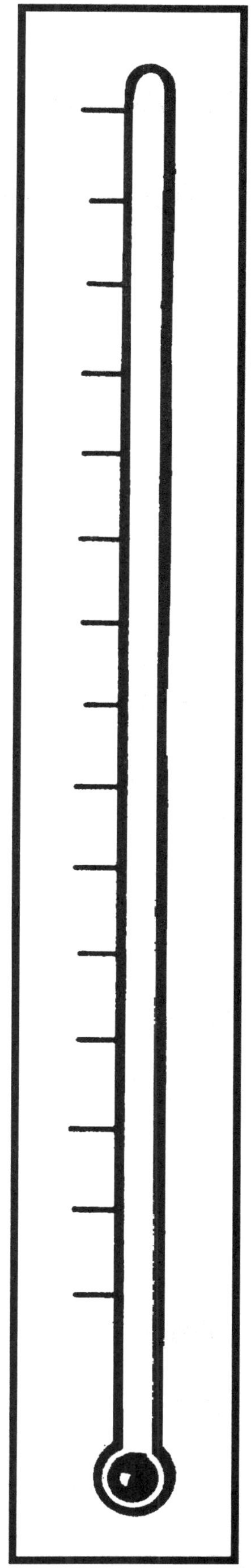

Summer

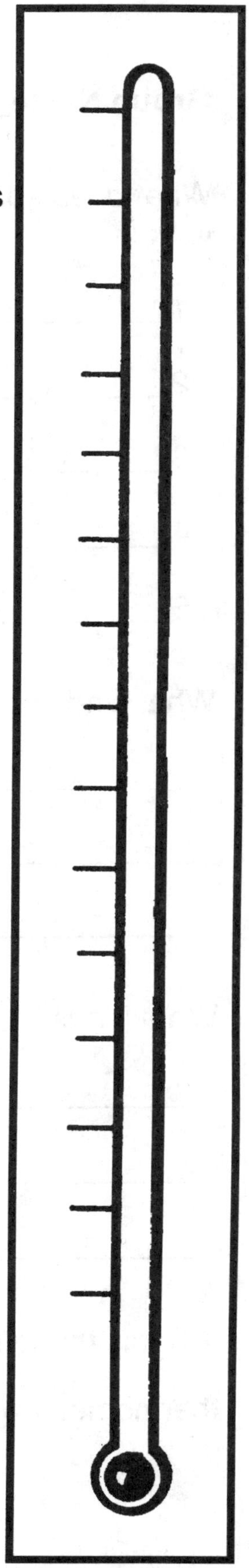

Group Name____________________________________

What does summer look like? Describe five ways summer looks to you.

1. ____________________________________
2. ____________________________________
3. ____________________________________
4. ____________________________________
5. ____________________________________

What kinds of clothes do we wear in the summer?

____

____

____

What kinds of weather do we have in the summer?

____

____

____

What is the temperature in the summer? Show it on the thermometer on this page. ____________________

 ©1995 Teacher Created Materials, Inc.

Fall

Winter

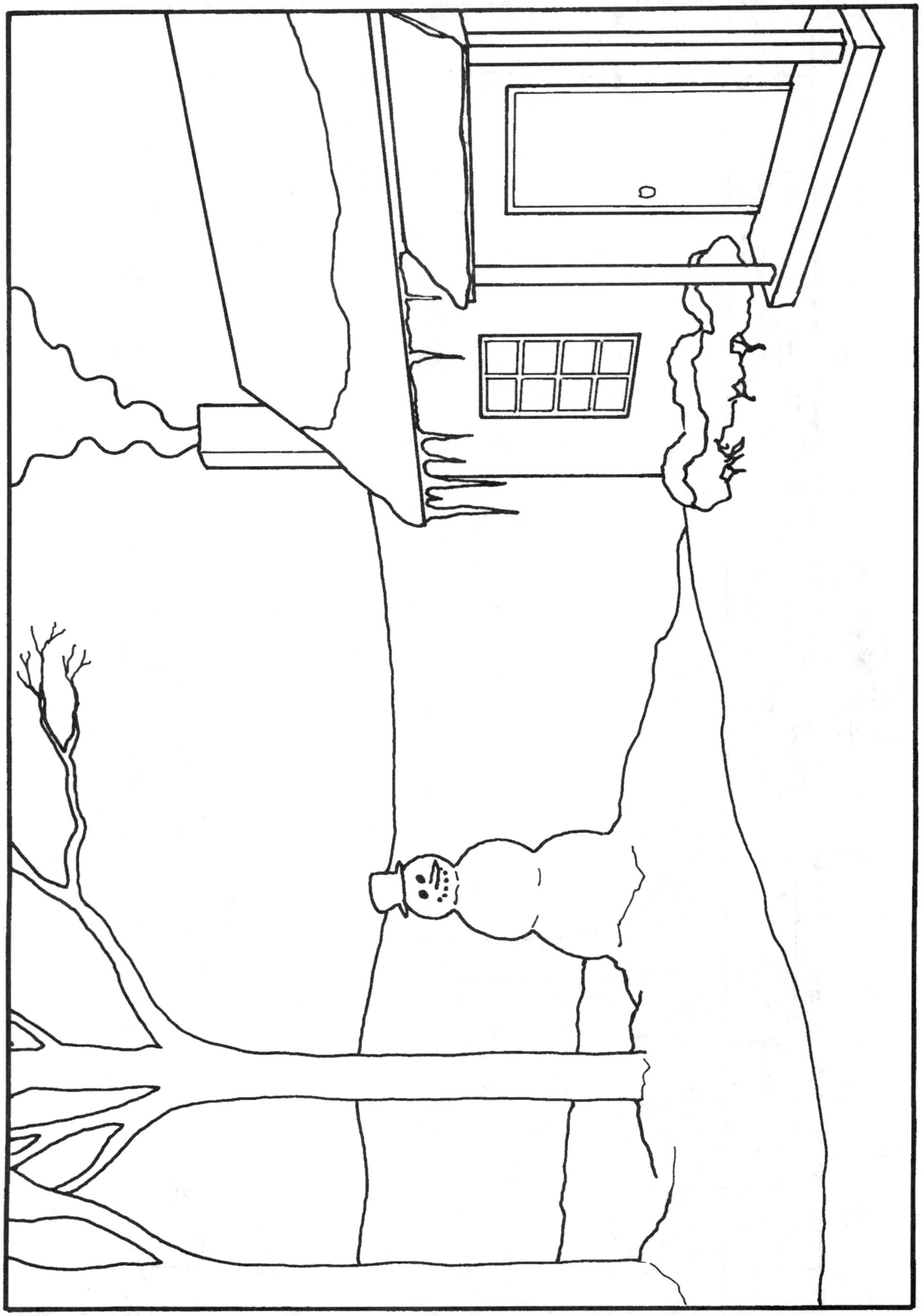

 ©1995 Teacher Created Materials, Inc.

Spring

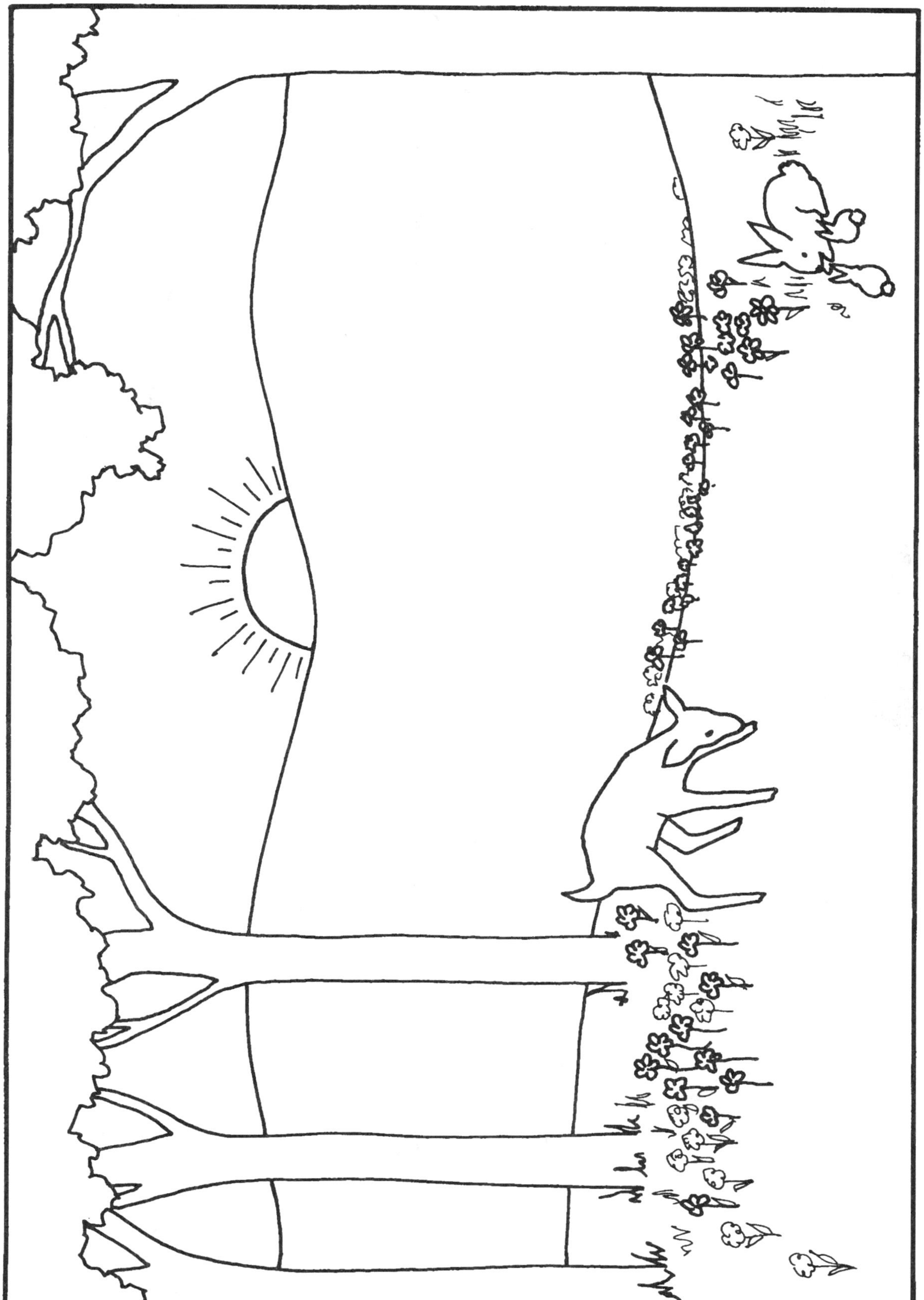

Summer

 ©1995 Teacher Created Materials, Inc.

Shoebox Weather Figures

Shoebox Planner

Group Name ______________________________

Which season will our group choose?

____

What materials will we use?

____

____

____

____

What jobs will need to be done, and who will do them?

____

____

____

____

____

Use the space below to sketch your scene:

 ©1995 Teacher Created Materials, Inc.

Shoebox Directions

1. Cut off one long side of a shoebox.

2. Line the inside of the three remaining sides with a seasonal scene that you have already colored.

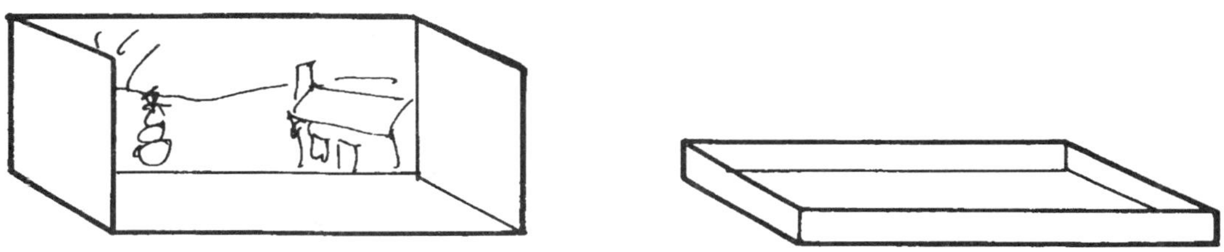

3. Add figures of people and any nature materials you want.

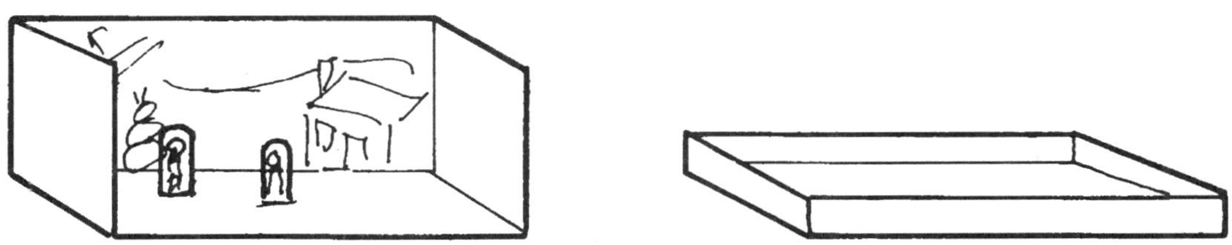

4. Put the cover back on the shoebox. You can now cover or paint the outside of the box.

Seasons Cookie Sheet

 ©1995 Teacher Created Materials, Inc.

Birdie Buffet

Purpose: to provide students with information about animals, especially birds, that stay in their area in the winter and to give the students an opportunity to observe and provide food for the birds in the context of a winter craft project

Skills: researching, observing, recording information, following directions, and experiencing a hands-on craft

Materials: large pine cones (one for each student), one large pine cone for classroom use, peanut butter, plastic picnic knives, bird seed, one small plastic bag with zip or twist closure for each student, one copy of page 139 for each group, one copy of page 140 for each group, one copy of page 141 for each student to take home plus one for each group for classroom use, one copy of the letter on page 142 for each student, one copy of page 143 for each group, a supply of reference books in the Science Club Center

Procedures: To begin this activity, hold a whole-class discussion about the animals that do not migrate during the winter months. Have students do the "Protecting Our Animals" activity page as a whole class. Discuss. Ask students if they have observed the birds that stay around their area in the winter. Talk about the fact that it is harder for birds to find food in the winter and what kinds of food they might need to help them stay warm.

Describe the pine cone bird feeder that the students will be making and display one, if you have time to make one ahead of time. Ask if anyone can tell why it has peanut butter on it as well as bird seed.

Have students go to their groups and, using the "Make a Birdie Buffet!" instruction sheet, have each student make a pine cone bird feeder. Have students cooperate to make an extra feeder for their group to use at school. (Enlist aides, parent volunteers, or older students to help with this project.)

Describe the idea of taking the feeder home and hanging it outside where it can be viewed through a window. (Students with pet cats should be careful to hang the feeders so that the birds will be safe.) Demonstrate the use of the "Birdie Buffet Observation Page." You may wish to make and distribute a copy of "Bird Illustrations" to each group to help with the identification process. Plan to set aside time for students to report on their observations.

To Simplify: Simply plan to do this activity as a cooperative craft project.

To Expand: Have students find out about the birds that do leave or migrate to their area in the winter, what kinds they are, and where they go or are from. Set aside time for students to share this information with the whole class.

Birdie Buffet *(cont.)*

Teacher Script: Today we are going to learn something about the animals that stay in our area during the winter. Let's complete this activity page together. *(Display "Protecting Our Animals.")* Have you noticed any birds? Do you know their names? Let's use our reference books to see whether we can identify some of them. *(Teacher allows time for the students to look through reference books.)* Jane has found one. How many of you recognize this one? *(Continue discussion.)* It is harder for birds to find food in the winter, especially the kinds of food they might need to help them stay warm.

We are going to make pine cone bird feeders to help these birds. Here is one that I made to show you. It is a pine cone spread with peanut butter and rolled in birdseed. Why do you think it has peanut butter on it as well as bird seed? (The fat in the peanut butter helps birds stay warm.)

Now you will go to your groups and, using the "Birdie Buffet" instruction sheet, I want each student to make a pine cone bird feeder. After your feeder is done, put it into a plastic bag and then work together to make a feeder for your group to observe at school. Ask the aides, parent volunteers, or older students assigned to your group for help, if you need it.

When you take your feeder home, remove the plastic bag and hang the feeders outside where it can be viewed through a window. If you have a cat, be careful to hang the feeder so the birds will be safe. Also, be sure to place the bird feeder near a source of water so that birds can have a drink as they feed from the pine cone. When the birds come to eat, you can write down what you see on this observation page. *(Display "Birdie Buffet Observation Sheet.")* Your group will also use one of these to log your observations at school.

Evaluation and Processing:

Give students time to report on their observations, both those made at home and those made at school. Encourage them to keep up this observation, using as many observation pages as needed. The completed observation pages make a good addition to the students' portfolios.

 ©1995 Teacher Created Materials, Inc.

Protecting Our Animals

Group Name ______________________

Here is a list of our five favorite animals:

1. ______________________
2. ______________________
3. ______________________
4. ______________________
5. ______________________

What can we do to be nice to animals?

____

____

____

How can we protect animals?

1. ______________________
2. ______________________
3. ______________________

Make a Birdie Buffet!

1. Get a large pine cone.

2. Put peanut butter in the cracks.

3. Roll the pine cone in bird seed.

4. Have a grown-up help you tie on a ribbon.

5. Put your birdie buffet in a plastic bag and take it home.

 ©1995 Teacher Created Materials, Inc.

Birdie Buffet Observation Sheet

Student's Name ______________________________

Group Name ______________________________

Date	Kind of Birds	Number of Birds	

Parent Letter

Dear Parents,

Inside this plastic bag is a wonderful treat for the birds that live around your home. This is a "Birdie Buffet." Your child made this to feed the birds! As part of our cooperative science unit, we have been studying various animals and their seasonal habitats. Your child has learned that birds enjoy bird feeders all year through, and some birds especially appreciate a little extra food during the winter months. This bird feeder is completely safe and natural and can be put up anywhere without fear of harming anyone or anything. I hope that you and your child have an enjoyable time talking about the cooperative unit and finding a great spot for your "Birdie Buffet!" Your child will also be bringing home an observation page so he/she can log sightings like a real scientist.

All that is necessary is to pick a tree or a nail where the feeder can be observed from a window. Loop the ribbon over a branch or nail. The birds will do the rest. You will want to place the "Birdie Buffet" high enough so that neighborhood cats and other animals don't destroy it. This will keep the birds in a safe place while they are dining out. *Be sure to choose a location that is near a source of water so the birds can drink as they feed from the pine cone.*

As usual, we encourage you to join us for classroom observation or as a volunteer. Please write your name and number below and return this letter if you wish to be contacted for any reason.

Sincerely,

____

- -

Name: ____

Student's Name: ________________________________

Phone Number: _________________________________

Best time to call: _______________________________

 ©1995 Teacher Created Materials, Inc.

Bird Illustrations

Pigeon

Hawk

Jay

Robin

Seagull

Owl

Sparrow

Hummingbird

Crow

Pelican

Canary

Parrot

Birdie Buffet Cookie Sheet

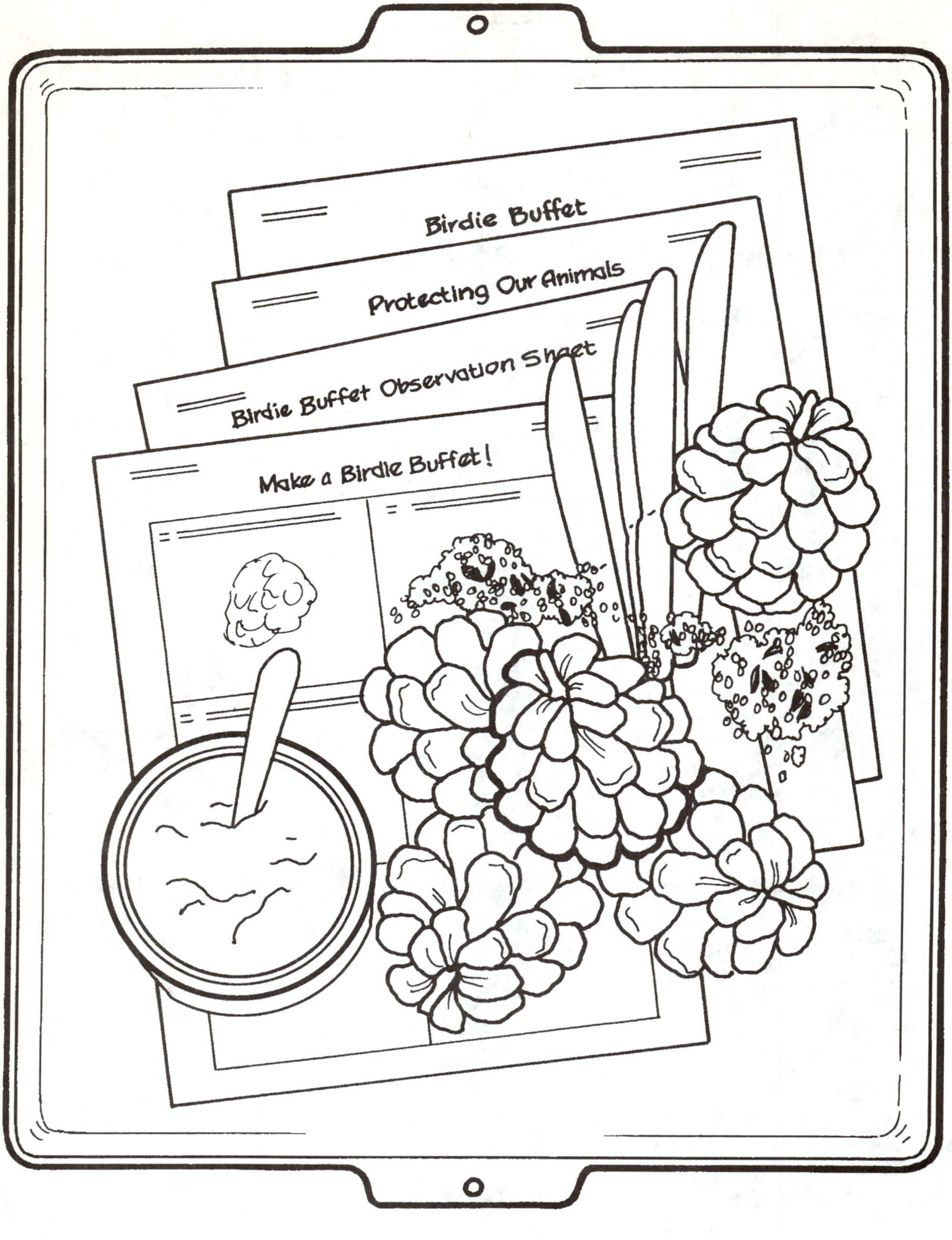

 ©1995 Teacher Created Materials, Inc.